Endorsements

As a missionary for twenty-nine years, I can attest to the fact that every entry touched on some experience or challenge I faced on the mission field. This is a valuable resource for a worker at any point of service and should be kept on hand as situations arise. Even now, as a retiree involved in stateside ministries, these devotions continue to offer wisdom and insight into daily challenges. In that regard, I would recommend this book as a resource for all, whether serving in an overseas setting or at any level of ministry stateside. It would make a great gift too!

NANCY BROWNING
Emeritus Missionary, International Mission Board, SBC

Carol is a long-time friend and colleague. When I first saw this book I thought, "This will be great for first-term overseas workers," but as I began to read it, I realized how wrong I was. This book is for overseas workers of any length of service. Almost daily Carol's devotionals spoke to me and where I am in my spiritual walk and journey as an overseas worker of twenty-three years. I highly recommend that every worker have a copy of this book to help them with the daily struggles of life on the mission field.

ELIZABETH GRAVES
TCK Member Care Field Worker

When Serving Gets Tough is wildly practical and deeply personal. It is a gift of encouragement and blessing for any overseas Christian worker endeavoring to proclaim the gospel faithfully while also living the gospel faithfully. Though Carol has a tremendous breadth and depth of knowledge and experience, which could easily and gladly inform her counsel to others, she instead magnifies the Word and points readers to the sufficiency of the Scriptures in all areas of "life and righteousness." And she magnifies our Savior, the one for whom we have left all things so the nations might know him.

TIM HOOD
President, CEO, Shepherd's Staff

Whether you're new to the mission field or a seasoned missionary, Carol's devotional will deeply resonate as you spend slow mornings with Jesus. Carol gets it. She understands the unique struggles you face as a missionary—problems with the kids, your spouse, the team, the culture, your spiritual walk, not to mention seeing little fruit as a result of your ministry. So before you decide to quit and go back home, you need to read this devotional. Grab your favorite cup of coffee or tea and soak in his presence as you read these pages. God will meet you as you abide in him, yielding eternal results.

DAVE JACOB
Founder and Director, Gospel Mobilization
Director of Mobilization, World Gospel Mission

In *When Serving Gets Tough: A Thirty-Day Devotional for Missionaries*, Carol Ghattas offers biblical truths and personal insights. Each day she asks questions and reveals concerns that resonate with my own twenty-seven years of experience of serving cross-culturally. She includes the resounding heart cry of missionaries walking by faith in challenging circumstances on the field: "Help Me, Lord!" then proceeds to offer Scripture and practical encouragement. I recommend this devotional to those serving across cultures—whether they're new arrivals or long-term sent-ones.

SUSAN LAFFERTY
Writer, Trainer, Mentor

Buy at least ten copies of this book to encourage and strengthen missionaries you know! Written by my long-time friend, Carol Ghattas, this book is part "pull up a chair and let's talk over some coffee" and a robust Bible study. Carol is like that big sister who's already been there, done that when it comes to international missions. She is unashamedly honest describing challenges and frustrations faced on the mission field. You'll feel like she's read your mind as she invites you to pray guttural prayers like *I am not cut out for this life. Would God really call me to serve him only for me to make a fool of myself by trying to speak such a language?* But then she swiftly ushers you into hope through a tangible injection of Truth. Carol is deeply biblical, and that's what I love about this little book! Each day's entry is bookended with Scripture and filled with more verses in the middle. You'll move from raw conversation with a wise big sister to hearing directly from the Lord of heaven's armies communicating with you, his beloved missionary servant, spurring you to keep running the race with endurance as he perfects your faith.

NATALIE (pseudonymn)
Friend, colleague, global worker among Muslims for over thirty years

As we prepare to go to the field, we believe we will be above any difficulties that will arise, but it doesn't take long for the issues of others to become our reality as well. Carol Ghattas does us a great service in this book, *When Serving Gets Tough*. She allows us to rush head on into the problem and to struggle with our situation. We are directed to the Scriptures and not allowed to sweep the issues 'under the carpet,' but to really deal with them. Her suggestions to action, confession, and forgiveness will allow the reader to honestly understand the problem but also to move on in a fresh pursuit of the calling that God has laid on our heart.

On the field for thirty-seven years, there was a book that I kept close so that I would walk through it every year. It always seemed to speak to me at just the right time. That will be the role of *When Serving Gets Tough*. Take the time to read the thirty chapters before you go. This will prepare you for the realities you will face once on the field. Then each year take time to refresh your heart and mind and actions, as Ghattas uses God's Word and real-life conversations to help you fall in love with the task that God has for you.

Ruth Ripken
Author and Speaker

When Serving Gets Tough

A Thirty-Day Devotional for Missionaries

Carol B. Ghattas

visit us at missionbooks.org

When Serving Gets Tough: A Thirty-Day Devotional for Missionaries
© 2024 by Carol B. Ghattas. All Rights Reserved.

No part of this book may be reproduced, stored in a retrieval system, or transmitted in any form or by any means—electronic, mechanical, photocopy, recording, or otherwise—without prior written permission from the publisher, except brief quotations used in connection with reviews.

This manuscript may not be entered into AI, even for AI training. For permission, email permissions@wclbooks.com. For corrections, email editor@wclbooks.com.

William Carey Publishing (WCP) publishes resources to shape and advance the missiological conversation in the world. We publish a broad range of thought-provoking books and do not necessarily endorse all opinions set forth here or in works referenced within this book.

The URLs included in this book are provided for personal use only and are current as of the date of publication, but the publisher disclaims any obligation to update them after publication.

Unless otherwise indicated, Scripture quotations are taken from the Holy Bible, The Christian Standard Bible (CSB). Copyright © 2017 by Holman Bible Publishers. Used by permission. Christian Standard Bible®, and CSB® are federally registered trademarks of Holman Bible Publishers, all rights reserved.

Scripture quotations marked NIV are taken from the Holy Bible, New International Version®, NIV®. Copyright © 1973, 1978, 1984, 2011 by Biblica, Inc.™ Used by permission of Zondervan. All rights reserved worldwide. www.zondervan.com. The "NIV" and "New International Version" are trademarks registered in the United States Patent and Trademark Office by Biblica, Inc.™

Published by William Carey Publishing
10 W. Dry Creek Cir.
Littleton, CO 80120 | www.missionbooks.org

William Carey Publishing is a ministry of Frontier Ventures
Pasadena, CA | www.frontierventures.org

Cover and Interior Designer: Mike Riester

ISBNs: 978-1-64508-594-2 (paperback)
978-1-64508-596-6 (epub)

Printed Worldwide

28 27 26 25 24   1 2 3 4 5   IN

Library of Congress Control Number: 2024946033

Dedication

In memory and honor of the men and women of God
who faithfully served over the decades as my prayer advocates.
I could not have persevered without their support.

The prayer of a righteous person is very powerful in its effect.
—James 5:16b

Contents

Introduction	10
Day 1: Who Am I?	12
Day 2: Did God Really Call Me?	16
Day 3: I'm Struggling, Lord	20
Day 4: What's My Purpose?	24
Day 5: I've Lost My Way	28
Day 6: I'm Tempted, Lord	32
Day 7: I Can't Handle This	36
Day 8: I Feel So Alone	40
Day 9: I'm Angry, Lord	44
Day 10: Do You Hear Me, Lord?	48
Day 11: My Marriage Is Suffering	52
Day 12: I Don't Like My Teammates	56
Day 13: Why Am I Stuck At Home?	60
Day 14: I'm Not Cut Out For This	64
Day 15: I Worry About My Kids	68
Day 16: I Don't See Any Fruit	72
Day 17: Why Is There So Much Evil?	76
Day 18: I Miss My Mom	80
Day 19: I Miss My Dad	84
Day 20: I Can't Believe What I'm Accused Of, Lord	88
Day 21: I'm Homesick	92
Day 22: I Hate This Place	96
Day 23: I Can't Afford To Keep Going	100
Day 24: These People Don't Get It	104

DAY 25: I Can't Learn This Language	108
DAY 26: How Can I Share If It Threatens Their Lives?	112
DAY 27: I Feel Spiritually Abused	116
DAY 28: Why Do My Kids Have To Leave?	120
DAY 29: I Can't Help This Bitterness	124
DAY 30: This Loss Is Too Painful	128
Conclusion	132
About the Author	134

Introduction

You are reading this book because you serve. You serve because you believed, at some point in your life, that Jesus is the Christ, the Son of God, and you committed your life to him. Everything changed for you—maybe not overnight, but over time—and in following him you heard his clear call to serve in his name. Perhaps that came through Christ's words spoken to his disciples after his resurrection and captured by Matthew:

> *Go, therefore, and make disciples of all nations, baptizing them in the name of the Father and of the Son and of the Holy Spirit, teaching them to observe everything I have commanded you. And remember, I am with you always, to the end of the age.* (Matt 28:19–20)

Or through those found in the book of Isaiah:

> *Then I heard the voice of the Lord asking:*
> *Who will I send?*
> *Who will go for us?* (Isa 6:8a)

However he spoke to you, echoing these or other passages of Scripture, you answered: "*Here I am. Send me*" (Isa 6:8b).

What you may not have realized at the time was how hard it would be. When we are caught up in the notion that he chose us, we don't always remember some of the other ways he spoke about the mission, such as in Matthew 10 and John 15:

> *Look, I'm sending you out like sheep among wolves. Therefore be as shrewd as serpents and as innocent as doves. Beware of them, because they will hand you over to local courts and flog you in their synagogues.* (Matt 10:16–17)

> *If the world hates you, understand that it hated me before it hated you. If you were of the world, the world would love you as its own. However, because you are not of the world, but I have chosen you out of it, the world hates you. Remember the word I spoke to you: "A servant is not greater than his master." If they persecuted me, they will also persecute you. If they kept my word, they will also keep yours.* (John 15:18–20)

Introduction

The Apostle Paul, in writing to Timothy, reminded him that "hard times will come in the last days" (2 Tim 3:1); and Hebrews 1:1–2 makes clear that the "last days" refer to the time beginning with Christ's first coming. It doesn't take long in our journey of service to realize the importance of these passages. When serving gets tough and we hit a brick wall, spiritually speaking, we need to go back to God's Word to renew our trust and regain our strength.

For this reason, I've written this book. I want us to be real as Christ-followers. Life in ministry is a challenge, and we all ask hard questions and face struggles along the way. Thankfully, the Lord has given us answers and words of comfort for times like these.

This book is purposefully devotional in nature, because, though I do give a few suggestions, my desire is for you to turn first to God. By letting him speak to you through his Word and in prayer, you can find your way forward. There is no one-size-fits-all solution to the trials we face in service, but there is one God who is waiting to help and heal.

There is also no right way to read this book. You can read it straight through, one day at a time, or jump around, reading the devotionals that touch a soft spot in your current struggles, while leaving others for later. The introductory paragraphs represent scenarios related to the topic of the day. Though written in first person, they are not all mine. Most are culminations of conversations and situations shared with colleagues and friends. I chose to keep them in first person for consistency and privacy.

As you read through each day's devotional and meditate on the Scripture presented, my prayer is that you will come to realize three things:

- You are not alone in your struggles.
- God can handle your cries and hurts.
- You can find comfort and help in his Word.

Reminded of these things, my hope is that you are encouraged to press on in service, recognizing that God works wonders through jars of clay. Nothing is too hard for our Lord, and he longs to strengthen your feeble arms and weak knees, enabling you to climb the heights to his glory.

He chose you for a purpose. May the days ahead remind you of his love for you and of his desire to work through you for the sake of Christ.

Grace and peace,
Carol B. Ghattas

Day 1

Who Am I?

> *For it was you who created my inward parts;*
> *you knit me together in my mother's womb.*
> *I will praise you because I have been*
> *remarkably and wondrously made.*
> Psalm 139:13–14a

"I used to be recognized in my community. Everybody knew me, and I knew everybody. I could easily check on people, get a feel for their spiritual health, and encourage or witness with ease. Nobody knows me here. I'm just another strange foreigner trying to fit in. The cultural differences make it hard to understand their issues and speak into their lives."

"The culture in which I serve is male-dominated in every aspect of life. Fitting in means I keep my mouth closed more than open and defer to my husband or other men in most situations. Not only does this mess with my mind, but since I lack a good grasp of the language, I have to stay quiet, because I have no idea what is going on. When a local pastor told my husband that he had such a wise wife, I realized it was because I had not spoken a single word!"

"I don't know me anymore. I was so sure of myself back home; so sure of where I stood with the Lord. Something's changed. I've changed. This new language and place of service have messed with my identity. I've lost myself in this constant striving to fit in—to become all things to all people for your sake, Lord! Is it supposed to be this way?"

Help Me, Lord!

Who Am I?

You are made by him.

Look at these verses again, this time reading them aloud:

> *For it was you who created my inward parts; you knit me together in my mother's womb.*
> *I will praise you because I have been remarkably and wondrously made.* (Ps 139:13–14a)

Do you hear the wonder in David's voice? There is true amazement in the fact that God knits us together. Every child is born with a special touch from the Lord of Creation. There is no happenstance in you—only purposefulness. There is nothing in this sinful, fallen world that can change the fact that you are a child of God. You are created and chosen according to his foreknowledge "before the foundation of the world" (Eph 1:4).

You are loved.

His love for us came at a great price, yet one he was willing to pay. He paid it while we were still sinners, undeserving of his redemption (Rom 5:8). His love is sure despite the current circumstances of our lives.

> *I have loved you with an everlasting love;*
> *therefore, I have continued to extend faithful love to you.*
> (Jer 31:3)

You are loved. Just as the people of Israel found the Lord's favor in the wilderness, you can know his favor in this wilderness of struggle. He sees you and hears your cry for help.

You are chosen.

> *But you are a chosen race, a royal priesthood, a holy nation, a people for his possession, so that you may proclaim the praises of the one who called you out of darkness into his marvelous light. Once you were not a people, but now you are God's people; you had not received mercy, but now you have received mercy.* (1 Pet 2:9–10)

Underline the words he proclaims here through Peter. What do these terms and phrases say about who you are? About your identity in Christ?

The Lord has called you—snatched you—out of darkness and into his marvelous light. Why do we seek the darkness when we are filled with the light?

We are God's. We belong to him. Even in our weakest moments and in our times of trial, we have full access to his mercy.

How do you respond to these words of truth? Who are you? What sin does this lead you to confess? Has your identity been lost because you had it in the wrong place or person? Did you lose your sense of self because you took your eyes off of the Lord?

Paul proclaimed to the people of Athens that in God "we live and move and have our being" (Acts 17:28). God has appointed the time and places in which we live so that we might seek him (Acts 17:26–27). As you live in your appointed time and within the boundaries where he's placed you to serve, may you live, move, and have your being in God, as his Spirit works in and through you for his good purpose.

Denying self is the price we pay.

If the Lord Jesus was willing to take on flesh that we might know God, should we not be willing to identify with those we're called to serve? Paul spoke multiple languages and lived among a wide variety of peoples—Jews and Gentiles. This former Pharisee of Pharisees willingly chose to leave his familiar and comfortable life behind for the sake of the gospel.

> *I have become all things to all people, so that I may by every possible means save some.* (1 Cor 9:22b)

Paul considered all he was—his entire identity—a loss because of Christ (Phil 3:7). Will you do the same? Resting secure in our identity while denying self seems like a paradox, but both are made possible in Christ. We rest in his love and press forward with purpose, while willingly abandoning self to his service.

For Further Meditation

Read through Psalm 139 and Jeremiah 31. Take in God's loving language to his people and hear his voice speaking love and restoration to you. Changing your dress or language can do nothing to change the essence of who you are in Christ Jesus. Find your balance by being anchored in him. Offer up your identity as a spiritual act of worship in order to do his will.

Day 2

Did God Really Call Me?

> *Brothers and sisters, consider your calling:*
> *Not many were wise from a human perspective, not many*
> *powerful, not many of noble birth. Instead, God has chosen*
> *what is foolish in the world to shame the wise, and God*
> *has chosen what is weak in the world to shame the strong.*
> 1 Corinthians 1:26–27

"I had a hard time getting home today, because I mispronounced the name of my neighborhood. The name of my neighborhood is very close to the word for naked in my new language—and that's what came out! I was so embarrassed. The more I grasp of this new language, the less I remember about my own. I butchered a Bible verse I was trying to share with someone, because my brain wouldn't let me translate it correctly from English. I make a pitiful witness."

"On my way home, I saw a man kneeling over a puddle of water and licking it up. I couldn't take in what my eyes were seeing. It seemed beyond hopeless. Where was God in that man's life?"

"I am not cut out for this. Would God really call me to serve him only for me to make a fool of myself by trying to speak this new language? How could he use me? I can't remember any of the verses I thought I knew. These people's problems are too much in the face of the trite gospel presentations I learned. I'm not sure I even believe what I'm trying to share. I'm so unworthy of this task. I've made so many mistakes already."

Help Me, Lord!

The call is real.

Jesus doesn't make mistakes when he calls people to serve him. Otherwise, all we'd have to do to find evidence is look at the twelve men who became his first set of followers. In the eyes of the world—even in the eyes of the modern-day church—they were a motley crew. Not one of them had all the qualifications of what we might think of as a man of God. This group was made up of at least one despised tax collector, zealots, hard-headed realists, and ordinary guys, including at least four fishermen; and yet, he still called them. Would he not also call us?

> *Go, therefore, and make disciples of all nations, baptizing them in the name of the Father and of the Son and of the Holy Spirit, teaching them to observe everything I have commanded you. And remember, I am with you always, to the end of the age.* (Matt 28:19-20)

We are all called to the same task. We are to make disciples by teaching others to obey the commands of Christ; yet, we don't do it alone. We do it with him. His presence, through the indwelling Holy Spirit, is with us always. He never leaves us or forsakes us. We may feel lonely in our obedience to the call, but we are never alone.

We are called to tell of his mighty acts.

Our job is to point people to Jesus. We do that by demonstrating his love in acts of kindness toward others and by sharing all his great deeds from Creation to Salvation and beyond (Ps 145:11-12). Is there anything good in your life? It's because of Jesus. Is there anything beautiful in the world around us? It's because of Jesus. Is there any hope for humankind? There is—through Jesus.

> *For we are not proclaiming ourselves but Jesus Christ as Lord, and ourselves as your servants for Jesus's sake. For God who said, "Let light shine out of darkness," has shone in our hearts to give the light of the knowledge of God's glory in the face of Jesus Christ.*
>
> *Now we have this treasure in clay jars, so that this extraordinary power may be from God and not from us.* (2 Cor 4:5-7)

He works things out as we obey.

Do we mess things up along the way of service? Absolutely. Does that mean he's not accomplishing his purposes through us? Not at all. Paul told the believers in Rome that "all things work together for the good of those who love God, who are called according to his purpose" (Rom 8:28). As you continue to read that chapter, Paul makes it clear that as God conforms us to the image of Christ, he glorifies himself through us. As we live, walk, and serve in obedience to Christ, God is with us and working through us.

God accomplishes his will through us, even when we don't see it. Your struggles with culture or language may be sending a message to a national that says, "That foreigner must really love my people to try to learn our language or to eat our food." They may never say it to you, but that doesn't mean that God is not using even your struggles to plant seeds of faith in the hearts of those who watch you.

He chooses the weak to reveal his glory.

Our "clay jars" (2 Cor 4:7) are evidence that this extraordinary power is not from us; and just as Jesus chose those twelve unlikely apostles, he also chooses us for a purpose. In the first chapter of Paul's first letter to the church in Corinth, he reminds believers that God's power is seen through that which man views as foolish. He purposefully chooses the insignificant and despised of the world—that's us—so that we have nothing to boast about in ourselves (1 Cor 1:28–29). Anything good that comes from our weak but faithful attempts to give witness for Christ is to God's glory, and his alone.

If we were great at this job of making disciples, then we might be tempted to take the credit for it and take God's glory for our own. Instead, it's our weakness, our frailty in carrying out the task, that keeps us not only humble but also in position to shine even more light on the person of Christ.

For Further Meditation

God is not looking for perfection but for faithfulness. Confess your sin of pride. Ask him to restore in you the excitement and anticipation of what he will do as you refocus in obedience to his call. Talk with your spouse or accountability partner about ways to press on in light of the Scriptures you've read today. Write out Psalm 145. Highlight or underline all the great things we can share about God. Use this psalm as a basis for prayer.

Day 3

I'm Struggling, Lord

> *Therefore the LORD is waiting to show you mercy,*
> *and is rising up to show you compassion,*
> *for the LORD is a just God.*
> *All who wait patiently for him are happy.*
> Isaiah 30:18

"It's not easy being a team of two. My husband and I are the only representatives of our organization in the entire country. We were given an orientation in another location, but no colleagues live here here to see the reality of what we're facing. Workers from other organizations in the country are here, but their approach to ministry is so different from what our group expects. The time we have with leadership is so limited. They assume we understand not only what they expect but what we are actually doing."

"I arrived on the field as a single man, and within a few months my supervisor was on furlough and another couple were leaving for health reasons. There is another couple in a city about an hour away, leaving me in this city with a single woman. Talk about uncomfortable. How am I supposed to handle life here without a real team?"

"I don't know what to do, and no one tells me what I'm supposed to be doing. I don't know where to start or how to use my time. I feel like I've just been dropped here without a safety net or an instruction manual."

Help Me, Lord!

Return and rest.

When we are stressed, we don't rest. Worry and fear rob us of sleep. These are natural emotions and struggles when we've just arrived at a new location, and they are exacerbated when we don't have a strong team or any team to help us. God longs to strengthen and guide us, even when we seek help from all the wrong places, as did the people of Israel. They were looking for help from Egypt, but God warned them, calling them back to himself.

> For the LORD God, the Holy One of Israel, has said:
> "You will be delivered by returning and resting;
> your strength will lie in quiet confidence." (Isa 30:15)

Our natural tendency is to quickly find a solution for our struggle. God's way is not like that. He wants us to remain calm in the midst of the storm, rest in him, and trust him to make a way in his time.

Find confidence in Christ.

When we're not sure what to do, we must stop and rest. Regaining sleep will help us to reset and refocus. That's why the next thing God tells the Israelites is to find their strength in quiet confidence. This is not self-confidence. We already know that's a bust. No, this is confidence in God—his purposes, his timing.

Our struggles with a lack of direction may be a temporary setback. When we regain strength and confidence in him, we're able to see things with new eyes—his eyes. From there, we're able to do the next good thing, which may be right in front of us or may require us to seek guidance from our organizational leadership.

The Lord waits to show mercy and compassion.

Fears flee and struggles lessen when we counteract the lies of Satan with the truth of Christ. His mercy breaks through the barriers of doubt, and he compassionately opens our eyes to the way in which we are to walk. When we rest in him, our ears are opened once again to hear the Teacher, in the form of the Holy Spirit, who speaks into our lives and enables us to take the next step in obedience.

That next step does not have to be huge. As a matter of fact, it's usually quite small, like cleaning your apartment and unpacking. Perhaps it's a walk to the grocery store and getting enough food to last a few days. When we've rested and refocused on Christ, we find the strength to progress in life by faith and not regress in doubt and fear.

Lies are noisy; truth is quiet.

Make sure what you're hearing lines up with the Word of God. When we turn to friends and even family at such times, we can get conflicting words of advice. A worried mother will always want her child to return home instead of face stress on the field. A friend might tell you to apply for a transfer if you're struggling without a team. These voices are not always from God, and they can clutter our minds and increase our stress.

Anytime Satan is at work to make us discouraged, it's hard to hear the voice of God. We ignore his Word and neglect the still, small voice that is showing us the way to go. That's why the verses of Isaiah 30:15–26 are so helpful. It's all about returning and resting, regaining quiet confidence in the One who is waiting to show you mercy and compassion, making his way known. Choose to rest in him today.

For Further Meditation

Read all of Isaiah 30, and then pour out your heart to God in prayer, asking for his favor and mercy in your time of struggle. Also, ask him to help you recognize the tricks of Satan to get you to go down a path of doubt and struggle, so that you can regain your way in Christ. As you pray, include your leadership and colleagues—that the Lord will fill them with understanding and wisdom to pour more fully into you during this season.

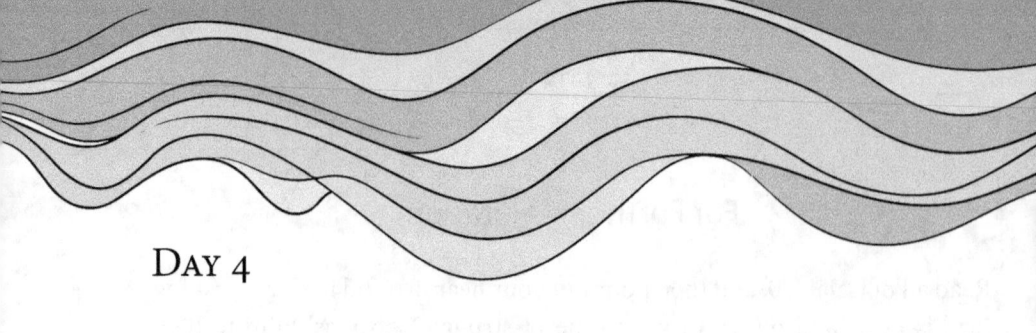

Day 4

What's My Purpose?

> How beautiful on the mountains
> are the feet of the herald,
> who proclaims peace,
> who brings news of good things,
> who proclaims salvation,
> who says to Zion, "Your God reigns!"
> Isaiah 52:7

———

"My wife says I've become a recluse. I go to my language class, but I'm finding it harder to get out among the people. The words I'm using don't fit with anything I feel like I should be learning. My wife will be doing the grocery shopping—So why do I need to know these words? I thought I was here to talk to people about God, not vegetables!"

———

"How could they ask me to take on the bookkeeping for the team? Really?! Now?! I mean, I'm just in my first term, still in language study, and trying to take seminary classes too. Just because I once worked for an accountant, they think it will be easy for me. Even though I'm only filling in for a colleague who's stateside, do they know how much stress this adds to my life?"

———

"I am so overwhelmed with surviving in this place. It seems like it's all I can do to keep my head above water between language learning, expectations of my team, and time with my family. Is this really what you called me to, Lord? Is this my purpose?"

Help Me, Lord!

Stop for a minute.

Twenty-five years passed from the time God told Abram (aka Abraham) that he would have a son and become the father of a great nation until the realization of the first part of that promise. That's a long time to wonder about God's purpose for your life. Perhaps you've been on the field that long and are still struggling, but most likely you've only been on the field a short while. Either way, we all go through this crisis of purpose—sometimes more than once. I mention Abraham because he helps us remember to take the long view of things, which is usually also God's view.

Reflect on other characters in Scripture who went through long periods of waiting on the Lord. Even those stories that may not seem explicitly like a call to ministry, like that of Hannah, are good to reread. She waited on the Lord for a child. God didn't respond to Hannah's prayer immediately; but when the answer came, she was faithful to follow through with her commitment to offer the child up for service. Her annual trek to Shiloh to worship God and to give her son a new robe seems insignificant in the grand purposes of God, but through her faithfulness a prophet was nurtured to lead a nation.

Be thankful in the midst of the struggle.

Reflecting on the story of Hannah in 1 Samuel 1–2, we find a beautiful model of how to press forward in obedience to God. Hannah prays to the Lord as she turns her only son over in service.

> *My heart rejoices in the LORD;*
> *my horn is lifted up by the LORD.*
> *My mouth boasts over my enemies,*
> *because I rejoice in your salvation.*
> *There is no one holy like the LORD.*
> *There is no one besides you!*
> *And there is no rock like our God.* (1 Sam 2:1–2)

As Hannah continues in prayer, she, like many others in Scripture, acknowledges the Lord Almighty as a God of action. He brings death and gives life; he brings poverty and gives wealth. He humbles and he exalts; he guards the steps of the faithful. As the God of knowledge, he weighs our actions. We know that he also weighs our attitudes as we seek to accomplish each day's work.

Not by might nor by power.

When we read and mediate on the prayer of Hannah, it's important to remember that it's not what we do that matters, but what God chooses to do in and through us and in spite of us that is all-important. We lose sight of our purpose because we think it's all about us. We think the mundane and sometimes painful tasks of learning language, shopping at an open market, and trying to keep our family from falling apart in a new culture aren't a part of his plan, but they are.

As we put one foot in front of the other in faithful obedience to his call, he's teaching us new things about himself and his Word. He's revealing to us new things about humility and trust. He's polishing and refining us to be more like Jesus.

His purpose prevails.

When we answer God's call to service, we carry with us a set of expectations as to how that will look upon arrival on the field. We plan and prepare, more often than not, based on those preconceived notions. Thus, when things don't go "as planned," we hit a brick wall.

Wisdom tells us that "many are the plans in a person's heart, but it is the Lord's purpose that prevails" (Prov 19:21 NIV). When you're overwhelmed, pray for *his* purpose to be accomplished, not *your* plans. In that state of surrender, you can be confident that in all things he will work for your good (Rom 8:28). Why? Because you were called to his purpose, not your own.

For Further Meditation

Use Hannah's prayer and Psalm 138 as models for your own prayer to the Lord. Focus on him. Ask the Father to fill you with his Spirit even when you're merely studying your vocabulary lesson, going to the market, or helping a new teammate learn the ropes. Bible commentators believe that Noah spent at least fifty years building the ark. Confess your unwillingness to be faithful in the mundane in order to fulfill his plan for your life.

As you go, ask God to use you, no matter the task, to proclaim the peace and salvation of Christ. Pray that your life of obedience will reveal to others that God is the ruler of your life. This good news that you have received is what you have to offer to them as well.

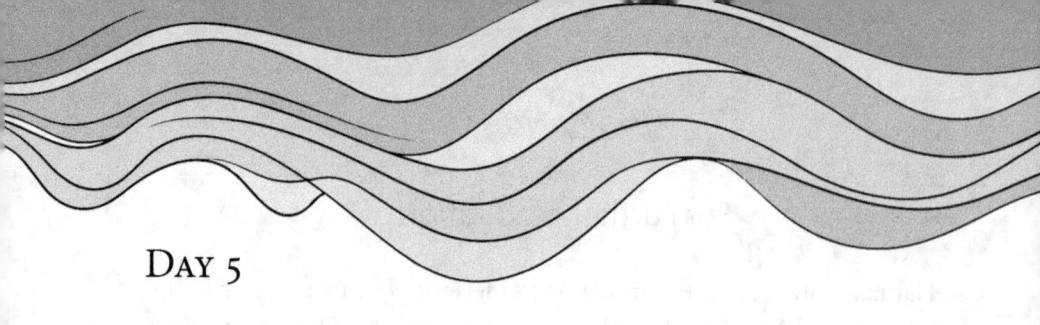

Day 5

I've Lost My Way

> *Some wandered in the desolate wilderness,*
> *finding no way to a city where they could live.*
> *They were hungry and thirsty;*
> *their spirits failed within them.*
> *Then they cried out to the LORD in their trouble;*
> *he rescued them from their distress.*
> Psalm 107:4-6

"This news is a shock. I can't believe my leadership is demanding that I come home for a mandatory training. I don't need that! Haven't they seen what I've been doing here? That training has nothing to do with my work. I know I'm called here, but this makes no sense. They were so supportive when I answered the call to lead this work, and now they are doubting it will even continue. If I go, there's no guarantee I can return."

"Is this really all you have for me, Lord? I felt like I was reaching so many more people back home. Here I've barely been able to share and I only have a handful to disciple. With their work schedules, our time together is sporadic. Am I making a difference?"

"I'm lost, Lord! I can't hear your voice anymore. I've never been this down or depressed before. When I left to obey your call, I was so full of purpose and certainty about what lay ahead. I knew you were in this and were with me. We would conquer the world together! Now look at me. I can't understand where you are in all this. Are you still with me?"

Help Me, Lord!

You're not alone in the wilderness.

There is no place too far or too deep for God to reach. You may be struggling to hear his voice, but that doesn't mean he's not here and near. Today we will walk through Psalm 107. Read the entire psalm and let God speak to you, but first realize this: the reason we have a psalm like this on which to meditate is because someone has walked this path before you. You are not alone.

Give thanks for a God who delivers.

Before we look at the ways we can miss the mark or lose our way, be thankful that God knows how to deliver. You may not be feeling very thankful right now; but when you start with thanksgiving, you will ultimately gain a grateful heart.

> Give thanks to the LORD, for he is good;
> his faithful love endures forever.
> Let the redeemed of the LORD proclaim
> that he has redeemed them from the power of the foe
> and has gathered them from the lands—
> from the east and the west,
> from the north and the south. (Ps 107:1–3)

Give thanks to the God who gathers. Thank him for gathering you from the grasp of sin when you were lost in the pride of self. Trust him to gather you again, to draw you into his presence.

Meditate on the ways we all wander.

As you read through the remaining verses of this psalm, think about this recurring phrase: "Then they cried out to the LORD." What were the ways some had lost their way?

(1) Verses 4–9: Some found themselves wandering in "the desolate wilderness" with a sense of both homelessness and hopelessness. That may be what you're feeling now. Not quite settled in your new home, while longing for one that's no longer the same. When we get to such a state, we're hungry and thirsty for things of the past. This stage of being caught in the in-between can lead to depression.

(2) Verses 10–16: Another way the people described in this psalm lost their way was through rebellion. They stopped heeding God's guidance. In most cases, rejecting God's advice means we listen to others. When we seek man's will over God's, we become indebted to him as master. Even in Christian organizations, God's will should trump that of man.

(3) Verses 17–22: Rebellion has consequences. When we turn our backs on God, it's easy for life to lose meaning; and we begin to withdraw from those around us, even on the mission field. Food loses its taste, and we grow weak in our isolation. Only God can save us from such a state.

(4) Verses 23–32: Finally, this psalm addresses the storms of life. We've answered the call to serve him among the nations, and we've seen him work in amazing ways. Suddenly a storm stirs things up, making us doubt our abilities and our call. Storms divert our attention from God. Only in acknowledging God and calling out to him can the storm waters grow still.

No matter the reason you've lost your way, cry out to the Lord in recognition of your trouble. You are serving the God who rescues (vv. 6, 20). He knows you. He sees you.

Consider these things.

The beautiful thing about realizing you've lost your way is that you realize it. If you refused to read this book or to reflect on the words of Psalm 107, then you would not be reaching out to the Lord. The good news is that you are—and he's been waiting for you to do just that. When we turn our eyes toward him, he floods us with memories of all the ways he's already proven himself faithful and good in our lives.

> *Let whoever is wise pay attention to these things*
> *and consider the LORD's acts of faithful love.* (Ps 107:43)

As you began with thanksgiving, continue with thanksgiving. Be thankful for specific ways God has worked in your life. Count those many blessings, and allow your mind and heart to focus on God's sovereignty, even when the world seems pretty messed up. As God leads you back to the path in obedience and blessing, he may be using you and the story of your life to shine the light on others who have wandered. Be a gatherer for Jesus.

I've Lost My Way

For Further Meditation

Spend more hours, or days, meditating on Psalm 107. It's rich and deep and useful for you and others. Ask God how he might want you to share its message with someone you know. Also, read Lamentations 3:22–26, reflecting again on the Lord's faithful love.

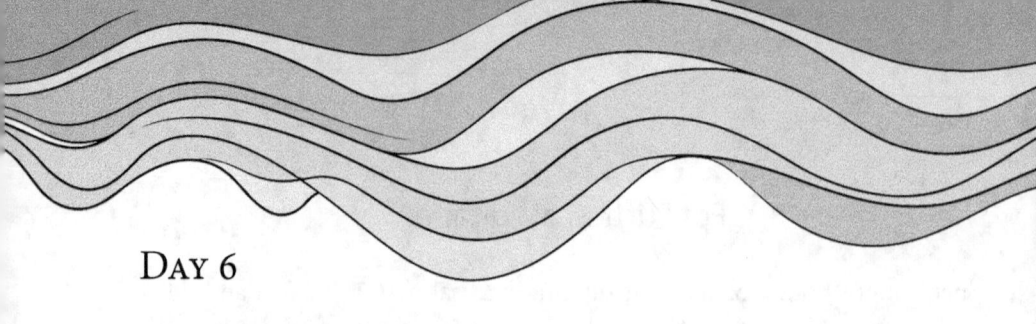

Day 6

I'm Tempted, Lord

*And do not bring us into temptation,
but deliver us from the evil one.*
Matthew 6:13

"I'm not sure what is happening. I never had this trouble before. Just because I acknowledge them and listen to their problems, several women in the church seem to have grown overly attached to me. One is even married! And I'm married! I don't know if I'm reading things right or wrong, but I do know that I've found myself thinking about a couple of these women in ways that I know I shouldn't."

"We ended up in his office with the door closed. I had noticed how his attentions toward me had increased in recent weeks, but I didn't think much of it. I know the rules, plus I know that there are way too many differences between us to make it work. I should know better, since a colleague of mine recently got sent home for deciding to marry a national. Wouldn't they treat me the same way? I can't believe he kissed me—right in his office! I feel like I've lost all credibility as a Christian woman."

"I'm not sure what to do, Lord. Satan seems to be throwing everything at me right now. He knows I'm weak in certain areas, and I wasn't prepared to have to face this after surrendering to serve you. I thought leaving home and committing to ministry would keep me from such struggles, but they're back big time! What will my spouse say if I admit I'm struggling? What will my teammates say?"

Help Me, Lord!

I'm Tempted, Lord

Even the giants of the faith struggled with temptation.

Choosing to follow Christ, choosing to step out in service to his call, doesn't mean we have a protective super-bubble that keeps us from facing temptation. As long as we live in this world and inside our temporal bodies, temptation will be a fact of life. Let's list a few of the temptations faced by those who have walked this earth before us:

- The temptation to take matters into their own hands: Abraham and Sarah (Gen 16, Gen 20)
- The temptation to set aside the promises of God for an immediate need: Esau (Gen 25)
- The temptation to take advantage of another person for something that God had already promised: Jacob, at the urging of his mother, Rebekah (Gen 27)
- The temptation to boast about God's favor: Joseph (Gen 37)
- The temptation to seek revenge: Moses (Exod 2)
- The temptation to want what others have (kings): The people of Israel (1 Sam 8)
- The temptation to give in to fleshly desires: David (2 Sam 11)
- The temptation to gain earthly power: Jesus (Matt 4)

There's only one person on this list who didn't give in to temptation. Everyone else—on this list or not—has yielded to temptation at some point in their lives. This doesn't justify sin, but it does mean that temptation is common to us all.

God doesn't leave us in the midst of temptation.

> *No temptation has come upon you except what is common to humanity. But God is faithful; he will not allow you to be tempted beyond what you are able, but with the temptation he will also provide the way out so that you may be able to bear it.* (1 Cor 10:13)

God's Spirit pricks our hearts and minds. When we are in relationship with God through Christ, it's virtually impossible to be blind to Satan's work in our hearts and minds. I like how the author of Psalm 73 says it.

He talks about how his feet had almost slipped, his steps had nearly gone astray. He struggled with his sin of envy for the prosperity of the wicked and arrogant. Instead of voicing his envy out loud, he confessed it to God. After his confession, God made clear the true destiny of those he envied, and the psalmist was humbled by his stupidity and sin. In his broken state, God took his hand and restored him with his strength.

Yes, our flesh and heart may fail—we may fall to the temptations before us, but God is our strength. He will lift us up, as we pour our hearts out to him.

God uses others to help us face the reality of our temptations.

There is no better example of how God reveals his presence in our lives at a time of temptation than in the case of the prophet Nathan confronting King David with his sin (2 Sam 11–12). God gifts certain people with discernment for a purpose, and sometimes that purpose is to speak truth to a person struggling with sin.

Nathan told his story to the king and then said these fateful words: "You are the man!" (2 Sam 12:7). God may use a spouse, a teammate, a national believer, or friend to confront you with a sin you think you're hiding. How will you respond? David immediately confessed that he had sinned against the Lord. Denial does no good; it only allows sin to fester and hinder us from serving in freedom. If you're facing temptation, who might be trying to speak into your life? Are you listening to them or avoiding them?

Don't keep silent in your time of temptation.

Psalm 32 reminds us of the importance of seeking help with temptations. There is nothing lighter than the release we feel when we've confessed our sins and found forgiveness.

> *How joyful is the one*
> *whose transgression is forgiven,*
> *whose sin is covered!*
> *How joyful is a person whom*
> *the LORD does not charge with iniquity*
> *and in whose spirit is no deceit!* (Ps 32:1–2)

Temptation itself is not the sin. Giving in to temptation is the sin. Confessing struggles to a trusted believer and to the Lord is the first step in the road to deliverance. As you confess, take the next step for continued accountability. Why are people who start weight-loss programs encouraged to work with a partner or a group? Because they know there will be temptations to eat things off the permissable list or to skip exercise. People go into weight-loss programs knowing their weaknesses and temptations. As Christ-followers, we should too.

God is by our side through his Spirit—encouraging, coaching, forgiving. The body of Christ is there, as well, for the same purposes of accountability and encouragement. No person is above or beyond the need for help to face temptations. Seek out the Lord in your struggles. And seek out a friend.

For Further Meditation

Reflect further on Psalm 73. Personalize it by making verse 3 express the temptation that you're facing. Write out verses 4 through 12 with more details of what your struggles are with the world and how they're upsetting you. Personalize and pray the verses. Use Psalm 32 to confess how giving in to temptation was making you feel toward God. Praise him for his strength and forgiveness.

Day 7

I Can't Handle This

> God has chosen what is insignificant and despised
> in the world—what is viewed as nothing—to bring to nothing
> what is viewed as something, so that no one may boast
> in his presence.
> 1 Corinthians 1:28–29

"New team members are coming in faster than I can keep up. I'm younger than some of them, and I'm the one who's expected to get them settled and then supervise their progress in language study. I really don't like telling someone older than me or who has been on the field longer than me what they need to do. How can a veteran worker be so needy?"

"I've been discipling a young woman. She's facing the pressure of an arranged marriage with an unbeliever. I see no good outcome for her, and I don't know how to give her advice. What do I know about such things?"

"I am so overwhelmed, Lord. Living here is hard enough, but I don't seem to be able to get anyone to understand me, even when I know what I'm trying to say. Then, the problems in our team and in the church are beyond my ability to help or fix. I just don't think I'm up to the job."

Help Me, Lord!

I Can't Handle This

It's good to know that you're not up to the job, because you're not.

Even Moses—the great Moses, the man who stood up to Pharaoh and led a throng of people out of Egypt, who survived grumblings and problems along the way and gave us the Torah—started out by pushing back to the Lord regarding his calling.

> "Who am I that I should go to Pharaoh and that I should bring the Israelites out of Egypt?" (Exod 3:11)

> "What if they won't believe me and will not obey me but say, 'The LORD did not appear to you'?" (Exod 4:1)

> "Please, Lord, I have never been eloquent—either in the past or recently or since you have been speaking to your servant—because my mouth and my tongue are sluggish." (Exod 4:10)

None of us are able to handle it—not life, not following Christ, and definitely not ministry! Calling out to God is a good thing. Getting to the end of our rope means we let go and let God. It sounds like a cliché, but it's our reality.

If we weren't working in our own strength in the first place, we wouldn't be out of it.

From the moment we declare our allegiance to Christ and "rise up with him in baptism," we put on the armor of his Spirit, which allows us to live by his power and might. How is it, then, that we feel God is not seeing our problems or hearing our cries for help? Isaiah reminded the Israelites, in Isaiah 40, that such thoughts were without cause. Didn't they know that God is never faint or weary, but always understands and hears (Isa 40:27–28)?

The Israelites complained, ran out of steam, forgot whom they were serving, and forgot their call, but God didn't let them rest in a pity party. He didn't even do that with Job—poor guy. No, our God is always reminding us of who he is. He is the Creator of all things. He is all-knowing and all-powerful. The first step in moving out of this place of suffering is to lift up our eyes and remember the God we serve.

Secondly, we have to remember this truth from God himself through Isaiah: "He gives strength to the faint and strengthens the powerless" (Isa 40:29). When our strength is no more, the Lord renews our strength with his. It doesn't take long for weariness to come when we are poured out in service for the kingdom; and when that happens, it's a reminder to stop and let him step in.

God uses our weakness for his glory.

We are chosen and blessed by God. We are also imperfect vessels through which Christ desires to work. By grasping our imperfections, our sorrowful estate in light of Christ, we allow him to shine through us. The Apostle Paul got it. He wrote in 1 Corinthians 1:20–31 that no one can claim he was called because of his wisdom or standing in society. In fact, the opposite was true. God purposefully chose the weak, insignificant, and despised to reveal Christ to the lost and dying.

God chose for the world to know him not through wisdom but through a powerful message that seems foolish, both because it goes against human wisdom and also because it is preached through weak, insignificant, and despised vessels—us.

Let go of the rope and rest in Christ.

Controlling takes effort, and when we strive to control, we burn energy that is limited by nature. That's why we can't handle it ourselves. Crying out to the Lord is good. We need to confess our exasperation. Then we need to stop and rest. Elijah, after the great defeat of the prophets of Baal on Mount Carmel, got scared by Queen Jezebel's threats and ran for his life. After traveling on foot about a hundred miles, he sat down under a broom tree and prayed:

> "I have had enough! LORD, take my life, for I'm no better than my ancestors." (1 Kgs 19:4)

What happened next? The exhausted prophet fell asleep until an angel suddenly touched him and told him to get up and eat the food the angel brought. Elijah ate, drank, and rested; and then the angel came back and "clicked repeat." That was enough for Elijah to walk forty days to Mount Horeb for an encounter with God and to receive new instructions.

Are you at the end of your rope? Rest; take care of yourself with the right kind of food, and rest again. Let the Lord speak into your heart and mind and then be strengthened for the next good thing he's asking you to do. As you go, let him have control.

For Further Meditation

Dig deeper into the life of Elijah. Consider the different stages of his ministry. Focus especially on 1 Kings 19 and think about the conversation Elijah had with God in that cave on Mount Horeb. Consider how having a helper in Elisha may have helped Elijah as well. Are you working alone? Whom might God be bringing your way to help carry the load?

Day 8

I Feel So Alone

> *Then they all deserted him and ran away.*
> Mark 14:50

"Our last team meeting was a doozie! Who knew that missionaries could have such tempers and be so territorial regarding issues? I expressed my opinion about how we are using funds with nationals, and no one spoke up to support what I said. I think a couple of teammates agree with me, but they didn't want to rock the boat. Now my team leader probably thinks I'm a troublemaker. I can't talk to my family back home about this, because they couldn't understand. I wish they'd at least check on me."

"It's not easy being the only single person on a team of couples. Several have been nice to invite me over for a meal or their family game night, but otherwise I'm on my own. I don't know the language well enough to really go deep into a relationship with another local person yet, and I'm not sure how close I ever will be, since they're at such a different socioeconomic level than me. I know guys are supposed to be able to make friends easier on the field, but it's not happening with me."

"Where are you, Lord? No one supports me or stands by me in this task. The conflicts in our team have torn us apart, and no one takes my side. No one texts or emails, and even my family forgets to call. And when they do, they don't ask about me but they just talk about stuff they're doing—which has no value, in my opinion. No one understands me."

Help Me, Lord!

He knows our pain.

Whatever the reason, perhaps today you feel isolated, deserted, and alone. Thankfully, we have a Savior who can sympathize even in this, since he alone carried the burden of his mission. Even though his disciples were with him 24-7 for three years, they didn't get it; they didn't understand his purpose. They couldn't stay awake while he poured his heart out to the Father, nor did they stand with Jesus as he was taken away by armed men. He alone carried the burden of our sin. He alone bore the cross, enduring suffering and death on our behalf. He did all this without sinning. He also showed us what to do when we become overwhelmed in our isolation.

Cry out to the Lord.

From fasting forty days in the wilderness at the beginning of his ministry (Matt 4:1–11) to the garden of Gethsemane and everywhere in between, Jesus took his suffering to the Father in prayer. That is crucial at this point in your life, and I'm grateful you're reading this chapter instead of sitting alone in your trial, because that means you're reaching out for help.

God alone is our refuge in times of trial. David was sitting in a cave when he recorded this prayer:

> *Look to the right and see:*
> *no one stands up for me;*
> *there is no refuge for me;*
> *no one cares about me.*
> *I cry to you, LORD;*
> *I say, "You are my shelter,*
> *my portion in the land of the living."*
> *Listen to my cry,*
> *for I am very weak.* (Ps 142:4–6a)

Satan uses the trial of isolation to tempt us to turn inward, to lash out at God and others, thinking no one cares. Through the trial, God wants to grow our faith and teach us new things about his presence. He is faithful to be with us even when we might be physically and emotionally alone. For these reasons, it's crucial to follow the examples of David and Christ Jesus in turning our eyes and minds upward toward the Father. Once we cry out to him and focus on him, we are better able to focus, once again, on the next good thing he's prepared for us to do.

Find your spacious place.

> *He reached down from on high*
> *and took hold of me;*
> *he pulled me out of deep water.*
> *He rescued me from my powerful enemy*
> *and from those who hated me,*
> *for they were too strong for me.*
> *They confronted me in the day of my calamity,*
> *but the LORD was my support.*
> *He brought me out to a spacious place;*
> *he rescued me because he delighted in me.* (Ps 18:16–19)

Psalm 18 has become my go-to psalm for comfort and guidance in seasons of trial. David wrote it at a time when King Saul, intent on his destruction, was actively searching for him. As we serve the Lord, we have an enemy who is constantly at work to derail and destroy us and our efforts for the kingdom. He uses these times of loneliness to prey on our hearts and minds.

As you turn to God for reassurance and peace, also seek out extended periods of quiet and rest. Pulling away from the busyness of ministry for a few days, or weeks, can help you gain perspective and refocus on God's purpose for your life. Find your "spacious place" and let God speak into your loneliness.

Keep an outward outlook.

As you turn your face toward God in prayer, he can help you maintain an outward focus in life. In your loneliness, have you neglected to pray for others? Praying for those around us lessens our tendency to think only of ourselves.

As you begin praying, let those prayers move you to action. Serving others in word and deed restores balance in our purpose and keeps us from sliding into the depression that loneliness can sometimes bring. Look up and out and you'll soon find the Lord pouring his healing balm into your heart and soul.

I Feel So Alone

For Further Meditation

Break down Psalm 18 into portions for daily reflection. Pray the verses and ask God to convict you of areas where you haven't given him full control or trusted him completely. Read Psalm 142. Seek the Lord's guidance for how to be vulnerable to family and colleagues in sharing your need for fellowship and encouragement.

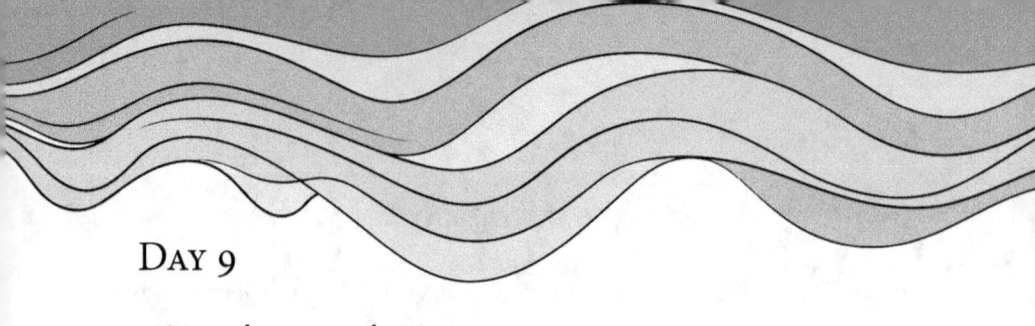

Day 9

I'm Angry, Lord

Be angry and do not sin. Don't let the sun go down on your anger, and don't give the devil an opportunity.
Ephesians 4:26–27

"I've seen it all. People who have lost their jobs, been ostracized from their families, imprisoned, and even killed—for what? Trusting their lives to Christ. One brother, even as he lay dying from cancer in the hospital, was forced to endure the screams of his family to denounce Christ and say the word of witness as a Muslim. At a time when he sought only comfort and love, he turned his head away from family to be welcomed into the arms of his Savior. I shouldn't be surprised. In a place of such darkness, hatred reigns. You can see it in the way they treat each other and in the way they drive. It's all about what they can get away with when God is not watching."

"I know this sounds petty, but I'm so tired of being taken advantage of as a foreigner. If I don't do the math in my head, the vegetable vendor always overcharges. I argued with a taxi driver last week when he tried to charge some visiting volunteers almost double for the fare. I told him he should be ashamed of himself, charging them more just because they were from America. I think I shocked the women with my outburst, but I couldn't let it go."

"My blood is boiling because of the injustice I see. It's not right that a person must face such abuse and danger simply for choosing to follow Christ. When I look at this people and this country, I am overwhelmed by the evil intent in their hearts. They do it to each other, and they do it to me, a guest in their land. Just because I look different or don't speak their language well, they take advantage of me. I'm sick of this."

Help Me, Lord!

Be angry, but don't sin.

When we leave our home environment to serve the Lord in a new place or country, I don't think any of us expect an emotion like anger to sometimes take over. We are Christians, after all, and our hearts and motives are pure in our desire to serve. There are many reasons for anger to rise to the surface and become a hindrance to our faith and relationships with others.

- Anger over the loss of self-sufficiency. This one is the most subtle and difficult to detect, but it's widespread among cross-cultural workers.
- Anger over the rampant injustice among the people we serve. While we knew injustice existed in our hometown or home country, it becomes much more evident when we move to a new location or are among a people without strong Christian values.
- Anger over the harm brought upon those who do step out in faith to Christ. When new believers lose their job, are kicked out of their home, or even killed, a righteous anger rises in us—alongside a guilty anger as well.
- Anger over our own failings. It's amazing how quickly we discover that God has chosen an imperfect vessel for this ministry.

These few examples may or may not reflect the cause of your anger, so I encourage you to verbalize the reason to the Lord or record it in your journal. Recognizing the reason you're mad is the first step toward avoiding sin in your anger.

Don't fret—Turn from anger.

In Psalm 37, David wrote that we should not be angered or agitated by evildoers, nor should we envy wrongdoers who never seem to face justice for their deeds. As with all men, their days are numbered; so we should trust the Lord and do good.

> Refrain from anger and give up your rage;
> do not be agitated—it can only bring harm.
> For evildoers will be destroyed,
> but those who put their hope in the LORD
> will inherit the land. (Ps 37:8–9)

When we're angry over the deeds of others, God tells us to stop fretting about them. An easy way to know if we're sinning in our anger is to see if we're obsessed by what we see as an act of evil or injustice. Obsessing is another way of fretting. We can't stop thinking about it. We worry about it. Anytime we do that, we're not trusting God for the person or situation; we're holding it all ourselves and letting anger build.

Trust—Turn to God.

The antidote to anger is to trust in the Lord, delight in the Lord, commit our way before the Lord, and be still before him; waiting patiently for him to take care of the wicked. In all that, we refrain from anger. Anger has no hold on us when we trust the Lord. I love verse 8 of this psalm: "Refrain from anger and give up your rage; do not be agitated—it can only bring harm."

When we allow anger to lead to rage, we become agitated. Agitation harms us emotionally and physically, and it leads to wrong words and actions toward others, which harms them. I'd like to say that we should just nip anger in the bud, but I know it's not that easy. No human anger management is. God's way is always best, because he has better plans for us.

> *Watch the blameless and observe the upright,*
> *for the person of peace will have a future.* (Ps 37:37)

Refrain from anger and be a person of peace with a hopeful future. When we live as persons of peace among the nations, people take note. The peaceful person draws others to the source of peace—Jesus Christ.

For Further Meditation

As you think about the source of the anger you carry, take time to confess your anger before the Lord. Seek his help and guidance in letting go and letting him carry this load. Meditate on the verses of Psalm 37 and use them as part of your prayers in dealing with this anger. Rest in his peace.

Day 10

Do You Hear Me, Lord?

> *LORD, I call on you; hurry to help me.*
> *Listen to my voice when I call on you.*
> Psalm 141:1

"I thought arrival on the mission field would end the cycle of illness that has plagued our family; but no. It's not enough that I was diagnosed with cancer twice before the age of thirty. Now our youngest daughter has been diagnosed with type 1 diabetes at the tender age of ten. Our son had a terrible accident playing soccer, and my husband and I have both had some very weird illnesses that were not easily diagnosed or treated. I don't know if it's this country or if we're just cursed. Everyone we know is praying for our healing, but I'm sure they are getting tired of our emails that have "Please pray" in the subject line, because they are likely wondering, "What's wrong with that family now?""

"When will someone accept Christ? I've prayed and spread the seed as always, but nothing takes. I was much more successful in my home country. Are you not hearing my cries for these people, God? Don't you want them to be saved?"

"I have no idea if my prayers are going anywhere. I'm asking the Lord; but I don't know if he's hearing, because I know he's definitely not answering. My family can't seem to get out of this cycle of sickness. I'm not seeing any fruit in my work. I'm seeking God's guidance and direction on so many important matters, but I hear no voice."

Help Me, Lord!

An unlikely name.

I am drawn to Scripture when I struggle with prayer, because I know the problem isn't prayer but my attitude toward God. In my hurry to have an answer, I've forgotten who he is—the God who hears. I start with the most insignificant of persons: Hagar, an Egyptian (not a Jew) and a slave (not a free person). She had been drawn into a family drama, not of her own making, by a barren woman who gave up on God in her rush to have a prayer answered (Gen 16).

After becoming pregnant by her master, Hagar is mistreated by her mistress, so she flees to escape. There is no reason for the God of Creation to care for such a woman or the child she bore; after all, she's not Abram's wife, nor is the child the son of the promise. But the Lord does appear to her and hears her; and when she obeys and returns, she names the son she delivers *Ishmael.*

God hears.

The same God who heard Hagar's cry hears our cries to him in prayer. We see the struggles even in a man after God's own heart. In the fourth psalm, David calls to the Lord, because he has experienced the graciousness of the Lord in answering prayers of the past. He has a history with the God who hears.

> *Answer me when I call,*
> *God, who vindicates me.*
> *You freed me from affliction;*
> *be gracious to me and hear my prayer.*
> *How long, exalted ones, will my honor be insulted?*
> *How long will you love what is worthless*
> *and pursue a lie?* (Ps 4:1–2)

As David called out to the Lord, he wanted quick answers, but he was also willing to acknowledge God and what he had already done for him. As we pray, we remember and voice what we know to be true of God, both from his Word and from our journey with him.

When we acknowledge that we are lifting our prayer to the God who hears, we avoid sinning in our anger over any unanswered prayers with which we struggle. In doing that, we can reflect in our heart (Ps 4:4), trust in the Lord (v. 5), and lie down and sleep in peace (v. 8). We may not yet have the answer we're seeking, but we have kept the channels of communication open with the One who hears.

God is in control.

When we pray for a quick answer, what we are really praying for is *our* answer. We want what we want, and God should give it to us, because we're his children or because he's a loving God. In reality, it's about what God wants, not what we want—and what God wants is always in our best interest, even if it doesn't look like it at the moment.

How can we share Christ with others and teach them about the joy of praying to a God who hears, if we are not exercising that trust in the God of all Creation? When God says yes to our prayer, do we give him credit and praise? When God says no, do we trust his will over our own? When God says wait, do we rest and continue doing the next good thing he's prepared for us to do while we wait? Are we showing others that we are at peace with serving without controlling? Pray this psalm:

> *I lift my eyes toward the mountains.*
> *Where will my help come from?*
> *My help comes from the LORD,*
> *the Maker of heaven and earth.*
>
> *He will not allow your foot to slip;*
> *your Protector will not slumber.*
> *Indeed, the Protector of Israel*
> *does not slumber or sleep.*
>
> *The LORD protects you;*
> *the LORD is a shelter right by your side.*
> *The sun will not strike you by day*
> *or the moon by night.*
>
> *The LORD will protect you from all harm;*
> *he will protect your life.*
> *The LORD will protect your coming and going*
> *both now and forever.* (Ps 121)

Where does your help come from? From the Lord, who protects your coming and going. Lean into him and the truth of his care for you. Lean into the God who hears and answers.

For Further Meditation

Use either Psalm 4 or 121 for deeper engagement in prayer in the coming days. Confess to the Lord when you have tried to control his answers to your requests and commit to releasing answers to his will in the future. Gather others to pray with you regarding areas where you are burdened for an answer, while continuing to trust his timing and purposes.

Day 11

My Marriage Is Suffering

"Haven't you read," he replied, "that he who created them in the beginning made them male and female, and he also said, 'For this reason a man will leave his father and mother and be joined to his wife, and the two will become one flesh'? So they are no longer two, but one flesh. Therefore, what God has joined together, let no one separate."
Matthew 19:4–6

"We had such a strong marriage before coming overseas. I'm not sure what's happened. We're both facing the same issues with learning the language and adjusting to the culture. Somewhere along the way, we stopped talking. When I come home late from an outreach visit, she's already in bed asleep. Our sex life is almost nil, because we're keeping such weird hours and are exhausted more often than not. I know she's trying to send me signals; but since it's without words, I'm not getting it. I'm so frustrated right now."

"My husband has no idea what I'm going through. He's out all the time 'doing ministry' or having people in the house at all hours, expecting me to serve them. He doesn't let me know when someone's coming, so I'm often caught without a cake or cookies to serve them. His only idea of intimacy is sex; and when I'm mad at him, I just don't feel like providing for his needs. Besides, does he ever ask me what I need? Doesn't he know I'm an introvert and could really use a day of quiet?"

"I know what the Bible says. I know what Jesus says. It's not supposed to be this way. We are in ministry! How can everything be falling apart between us? I'm not sure who this person is anymore. When did we grow so far apart?"

Help Me, Lord!

We go back to go forward.

I wonder why a bunch of Pharisees chose to test Jesus by pulling out a question about divorce. Maybe one of them was struggling with his own marriage and wanted to see what this radical rabbi would say. Jesus doesn't directly answer the question (he rarely does), but instead takes them to what God had already said about the matter. He took them back to the beginning.

The God who made us for relationship with him also made us for relationship with each other, and marriage is the cornerstone of all other relationships in society today. Male and female leave their fathers and mothers to become one flesh as husband and wife. The ones God brings together, no one should separate.

As Christ-followers, we need to first be clear about what marriage is and who established it. We go back to the beginning in Scripture and also in our relationship. When you're in the midst of the pain, stop and remember. As they prepared to go into the Promised Land, Moses told the Israelites to be a people who remember. We, too, should be people who remember. Remembering keeps us from forgetting—forgetting how we met, how we felt about each other, what God was saying to each of us before we committed to marriage, and how he showed us more of himself after we married.

We remember what's required of us in marriage.

There is no easy road in marriage. It takes work. After all, we're talking about two completely different people spending all their time together. Scripture has some very clear guidelines on marriage. Here are a few:

> *Wives, submit yourselves to your husbands, as is fitting in the Lord. Husbands, love your wives and don't be bitter toward them.* (Col 3:18–19)
>
> *But because sexual immorality is so common, each man should have sexual relations with his own wife, and each woman should have sexual relations with her own husband.* (1 Cor 7:2)
>
> *Do not deprive one another—except when you agree for a time, to devote yourselves to prayer. Then come together*

> *again; otherwise, Satan may tempt you because of your lack of self-control.* (1 Cor 7:5)
>
> *Marriage is to be honored by all and the marriage bed kept undefiled, because God will judge the sexually immoral and adulterers.* (Heb 13:4)

The reason I focus on verses related to sex is because when a marriage suffers, the couple's sex life is always involved. Ministry, especially if it involves living cross-culturally, puts extra stress on marriage. Men and women feel the pressure of expectations of colleagues, churches, nonbelievers, and even themselves about what ministry looks like and how much time is needed to pour into the lives of others. If expectations are unrealistic (both from others and ourselves), we stress out. We allow no margin for error, rest, family, and especially not for marriage.

This impacts how the husband may enter the marriage bed and how the wife reacts. Sexual needs go unmet or are abused, which leads to rejection and hurt.

God has a great book for marriage therapy.

Not only do we need to go back to the beginning to remember what marriage is meant to be and how ours was in the beginning, but we also should speak to each other with loving words. Marital stress impacts how we speak to our spouse, and often it's with ugly or hurtful words. Sometimes it leads to silence—a complete breakdown in communication. When we can't find our own words, God provides some we can use.

Take time away from the noise of ministry and life, find a quiet place to be together, and talk. Remember together how you were in the beginning, talk about the current struggles, and then commit to speaking love to each other through the words of the Song of Songs. Words like this:

> *Oh, that he would kiss me with the kisses of his mouth!* (Song 1:2).
>
> *How beautiful you are, my darling. How very beautiful!* (Song 1:15).
>
> *Set me as a seal on your heart, as a seal on your arm.* (Song 8:6a).

While you may need to have a third party speak into your marriage through professional counseling, I encourage you, as a couple, to start with God's Word. Let God speak into your marriage before any other voice enters into the conversation.

For Further Meditation

As you pray daily for and with your spouse, use the Song of Songs as a personal marriage retreat. Be creative in how you speak it to each other, and don't be shy. God created marriage as the most intimate of relationships because it reflects the intimacy of Christ's relationship with his bride, the church. Honoring God in maintaining a loving, growing marriage gives witness to others for his glory. Search out Scripture passages that describe your mate. Share them with each other and pray them over each other.

Day 12
I Don't Like My Teammates

> *After this, the Lord appointed seventy-two others, and he sent them ahead of him in pairs to every town and place where he himself was about to go. He told them, "The harvest is abundant, but the workers are few. Therefore, pray to the Lord of the harvest to send out workers into his harvest. Now go; I'm sending you out like lambs among wolves."*
> Luke 10:1–3

"We traveled to spend some time with colleagues in another part of the country, but that meant we had to stay with a couple who might end up as our supervisors in the near future. I would have rather stayed at our friends' house, but we didn't have a choice in the matter. The guy is alright, but his wife is just so overbearing. Would God really make us be on the same team? I feel for our friends, because they have to work with them now. If they're obviously struggling, how will we survive?"

"I can't stand my team leader! He is so opinionated and doesn't listen to what others are saying. He assumes we understand what's going on, when we are actually clueless. Doesn't he realize we're new?"

"Wow, I don't know how I ended up on such a team! If I had known the kind of people I was going to have to serve with, I'm not sure I would have come. It's so hard to be in fellowships or meetings with some of my teammates—they just don't understand me and look at things so differently. I have no clue where they're coming from."

Help Me, Lord!

The church is made of many parts.

Life in ministry is just a mini-model of life in the church. We are all different in our backgrounds, salvation stories, education, and spiritual journeys. It's easy for Christians who surrender to missions or other ministry to forget that we do not serve in isolation. We need others, and just as Jesus sent the seventy-two out in pairs, we too are paired and grouped with others who are called to serve the same people group, church, or city.

We also sometimes forget that *like-minded doesn't mean* "alike in all things." Another person who is called to work with animists in my city may have an entirely different view of how to reach them with the gospel. Team life requires us to listen and learn from each other in order to be most effective in our purpose.

> *But as it is, God has arranged each one of the parts in the body just as he wanted.* (1 Cor 12:18)

Read the entire passage of 1 Corinthians 12:12–19. You're on this team by God's design in order to exercise your giftings toward a common purpose. The ultimate goal is to bring him glory. As baptized believers, we are filled with the same Spirit, which helps our differences in gifting and service work as a unified whole under the leadership of Christ. We need each other to fulfill the purposes for which God has called us together in service.

Along with our differences and unique giftings, we also need to remember that we're all cracked pots—fallen human beings, saved by grace. Thus, we need to show grace to one another, just as Christ showed his grace to us. Look for the good and benefits gained through the differences you find in your teammates; they may offer you a perspective on an issue that you never saw before.

When relationships get rocky, turn to Scripture.

If personality conflicts make it difficult to talk to a colleague, the words of Christ should always convict and guide us.

> *By this everyone will know that you are my disciples, if you love one another.* (John 13:35)

Scripture reveals that one of the strongest witnesses to our faith in Christ is how we relate to one another as believers. When we show love, even across or despite of our differences, others see that we are his disciples. We must rely on the Spirit for unity in a general sense and also, specifically, to fill us with the love of Christ for our teammates.

> *Therefore, confess your sins to one another and pray for one another, so that you may be healed. The prayer of a righteous person is very powerful in its effect.* (Jas 5:16)

Prayer for our colleagues guards us from the temptation of judgment, comparison, and anger. Asking for forgiveness keeps our slates clean. Prayer also changes our attitude and helps us to see the other person as Christ does. Keeping a clean slate with teammates is crucial in maintaining a spirit of openness and transparency.

How might God want to use you in your teammates' lives and vice versa? Proverbs 27:17 tells us that we can sharpen each other in our walk with Christ. The Lord may use the different perspective of a teammate to open your eyes to a weakness or insufficiency in your own approach to ministry. As we speak Scripture to each other, our faith grows and matures.

Maintain a healthy distance from colleagues.

One of the struggles, especially with those serving in cross-cultural service, is the amount of time colleagues spend together. If you are a small group of ex-pats and have no other outlet for relationship, spending too much time together can cause people to get on each other's nerves. It's not really about not liking them—it's just that you see them too much.

> *Seldom set foot in your neighbor's house; otherwise, he'll get sick of you and hate you.* (Prov 25:17)

Find constructive ways to talk together about maintaining a healthy distance and allowing for you to have some privacy. This is hard when it relates to single roommates who don't have other ways to socialize; but through prayer and conversation, you can work things out. Make your needs clear, and your teammate will eventually come to understand the issue. Spending too much time with teammates can also affect families, if constant interruptions keep you from having family time or privacy as a couple. If necessary, use a team gathering to talk about how the group can work on understanding boundaries and maintaining healthy relationships.

For Further Meditation

Ask the Lord to give you specific verses to pray for in relation to a teammate with whom you're struggling. When we pray for others, our attitude is the first to change. Start by using one of the Apostle Paul's prayers for believers.

Day 13

Why Am I Stuck at Home?

> *A wife of noble character is her husband's crown,*
> *but a wife who causes shame*
> *is like rottenness in his bones.*
> Proverbs 12:4

"I began to question why I had even bothered to get a master's degree in theology if all I was going to do was stay at home. Before we had kids, I was still learning the language, so I really couldn't communicate with or disciple the new believers my husband was winning to the Lord. By the time I had mastered the language, I had our first child, with the second coming three years later. I know they are—and should be—my priority, but I don't see an end in sight. My mom isn't here to help, and my husband has no set schedule, so I can't depend on him to help either."

"I am so tired of these four walls, and I'm not thrilled about my kids at the moment either! Can't I have a break? My husband is out at all hours doing ministry, and I'm stuck here alone or with the kids. I didn't sign up for this. I want to be serving too!"

Help Me, Lord!

Your service is invaluable in his sight.

God established the marriage relationship in the garden, and from that first union every home has been built. The role of wife and mother has been central to the stability of every society since the beginning of time. When you feel like you're exiled in your home, remember God's words through Jeremiah.

> *This is what the LORD of Armies, the God of Israel, says to all the exiles I deported from Jerusalem to Babylon: "Build houses and live in them. Plant gardens and eat their produce. Find wives for yourselves, and have sons and daughters. Find wives for your sons and give your daughters to men in marriage so that they may bear sons and daughters. Multiply there; do not decrease. Pursue the well-being of the city I have deported you to. Pray to the LORD on its behalf, for when it thrives, you will thrive."* (Jer 29:4–7)

> *For this is what the LORD says: "When seventy years for Babylon are complete, I will attend to you and will confirm my promise concerning you to restore you to this place.* **For I know the plans I have for you**"—this is the LORD's declaration—"**plans for your well-being, not for disaster, to give you a future and a hope.** *You will call to me and come and pray to me, and I will listen to you. You will seek me and find me when you search for me with all your heart. I will be found by you"—this is the LORD's declaration—"and I will restore your fortunes and gather you from all the nations and places where I banished you"—this is the Lord's declaration. "I will restore you to the place from which I deported you."* (Jer 29:10–14)

We often quote verse 11 (which I put in bold) and apply it to whatever difficulties we're currently facing, while ignoring the context of the passage—which was set in the beginning of the Israelites' seventy years in exile. Right now you may feel like it's been seventy years since you've felt this isolated, but it's just for a season of life, not forever. Still, if you'll meditate on this passage you'll find that building houses, planting gardens, getting married and having children—all this is for the well-being of the place where you're serving. As you're in your home, pray for the people of your city and region. Your prayers for their good will be for your good.

God has plans for you, and they are good.

The time you have with your children is fleeting, and you cannot take back the moments you lose with them. Press into them while you can, remembering that many families in America are out "living the dream": working two jobs and allowing others to raise their children. You have the privilege of being the one to fill those blank pages with wisdom from God's Word and Christ's teaching, not from the world.

Your role in maintaining a home that is a place of peace for your husband and children is so very important. Don't think lightly of it—God doesn't. Remember how Paul honored the "sincere faith" of Timothy's mother and grandmother. These women were in the home, caring for their family, and yet their faith was recognized (2 Tim 1:5).

> *I know how to make do with little, and I know how to make do with a lot. In any and all circumstances I have learned the secret of being content—whether well fed or hungry, whether in abundance or in need. I am able to do all things through him who strengthens me.* (Phil 4:12–13)

God's plans for you are good—they are good when he has you nurturing and teaching children, and they are good when he has you ministering among other women or with your husband. The question is: Will you be content today?

Don't rush the seasons of life.

In our hurry to serve the Lord, we often miss opportunities he gives us in the season in which we are currently living. Rushing to serve alongside your husband, you may miss the questions your child is asking about God or faith. God made the seasons in nature, and they are indicators of the seasons of life through which we all must go.

Consider the words of wisdom in Ecclesiastes 3:1–8. What season are you living in today? Recognizing the temporal time of any season helps to release the stress of feeling trapped.

Connect with others in your area who are in the same season. Find ways to encourage each other, and consider getting together with your children for special activities and play dates.

For Further Meditation

Mediate on Philippians 4:4–13. Ask the Lord to give you satisfaction, whatever your stage of life or situation. Talk with your husband about what you're feeling in this season of life and see how he can help you find outlets for service that won't take you away from your primary roles. Pray for each other, remembering that he may be missing you as well.

If you're the husband and reading this chapter, ask the Lord how you can encourage your wife during this season and how you can help provide outlets for her in ministry.

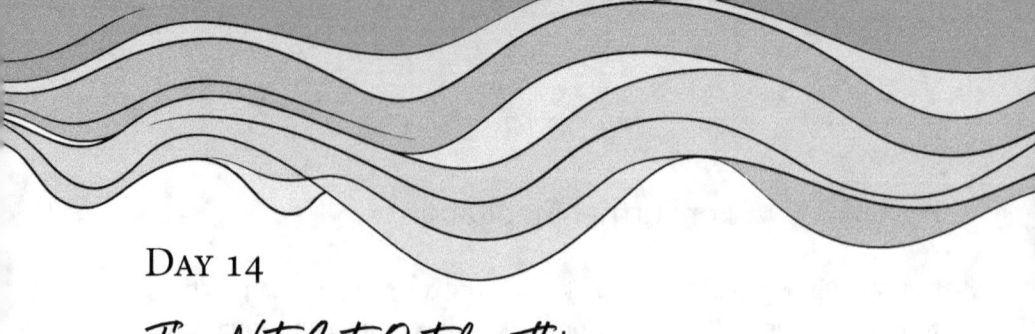

Day 14

I'm Not Cut Out for This

> So I take pleasure in weaknesses, insults, hardships, persecutions, and in difficulties, for the sake of Christ. For when I am weak, then I am strong.
>
> 2 Corinthians 12:10

"One day this last week, I was up at six and didn't get back to bed till two the next morning. I had to cook ahead for our boss and teammates who were coming to visit for three days. I taught a Bible study for some new believers who are going through things I could never imagine facing. They look at Scripture from a completely different perspective, because they are virtually blank slates in the faith. I ended up telling them I'd have to get back to them next week regarding several of the questions they asked. After a short nap, we left at eight to visit a family. The visit lasted five hours. Company arrives tomorrow!"

"My training is in ministry, not business, but I'm expected to handle personal and ministry budgets, purchasing of vehicles for the team, and signing contracts for renting apartments. They never prepared us for such things during our orientation. Don't they realize I'm not much of a detail person? I love the people we serve and every aspect of ministry, but this business stuff is beyond me. It's obvious my supervisor has caught on, because he's started sending some testy emails about things I've let slide in the office."

"I'm way beyond my abilities on this. I don't have the answers people are seeking, and I can't seem to find enough time in the day to meet all the needs thrown at me. They evidently didn't teach me the right answers in seminary, because what I thought I knew I'm not so sure of now. Maybe I'm just not cut out for this work."

Help Me, Lord!

I'm Not Cut Out for This

You're not the only one who has felt this way.

The demands of ministry and cross-cultural service can be overwhelming. Needs are flying at you 24-7, with no end in sight. Just when you think you've helped one person, another one knocks at your door. Everyone has questions and your answers are limited, and we're not even talking about physical needs.

I'm so grateful that Scripture is full of overwhelmed, inadequate people. An encounter between Moses and his father-in-law really speaks to this point. Exodus 18 is worthy of our study, as Jethro arrives for a visit. He'd heard about all God was doing through his son-in-law, and he wanted to get a firsthand view. He brought Moses's wife and sons with him, since they had been back at Midian for a while.

I love this story for how it lays out the encounter. Moses, excited to give his father-in-law a report, told him all that God had been doing. This made Jethro happy, and he praised the Lord and recognized him as the God above all gods.

Giving a report is one thing—seeing the work in action is another. That's what happened the next day, as Jethro watched Moses try to deal with the demands of the people. Moses thought he was indispensable, but Jethro simply saw a man, acting in his own strength and without seeking any help, and he told him so.

> "What you're doing is not good," Moses's father-in-law said to him. "You will certainly wear out both yourself and these people who are with you, because the task is too heavy for you. You can't do it alone. Now listen to me; I will give you some advice, and God be with you." (Exod 18:17–19a).

You can't do it alone.

This story is so important to study because it teaches us a lot about service. Moses, the friend of God and a great leader, was wearing himself out by trying to handle everything. God could have spoken to him directly, but instead he chose to speak through perhaps the only man who could make an impact—his father-in-law. Out of respect for his wife's father, Moses would be compelled to listen. I think they also had a really good relationship. We need people like this in our lives. These are the people to whom we should turn when we are feeling overwhelmed, because they will speak to us without any fluff.

In order for others to speak into our situation, we must pull back the curtain. Moses and Jethro had a special time of sharing all the great works of God up to this point, and that was great. Jethro rejoiced in what God had done and gave him praise as the God above all gods. However, it would be the next day, when Moses was letting his father-in-law watch him "at work," that the reality on the ground was made clear. Find that person who can watch you at work, if not in person, then through conversations. Share how you use your time each day, so they can help you see what you're missing.

Be open to change. Moses did not hesitate to take Jethro's suggestion, and he was better off for it. You need others to pray with you about how to find margin and better use of your time.

God is with us even in our trials.

The God who created and redeemed us is also the God who is with us when we struggle in service.

> *When you pass through the waters,*
> *I will be with you,*
> *and the rivers will not overwhelm you.*
> *When you walk through the fire,*
> *you will not be scorched,*
> *and the flame will not burn you.* (Isa 43:2)

Choose to turn to the One who has redeemed you for a purpose. This verse does not say *if* we pass through the waters, but *when* we do so. Trials are bound to come; they cannot be avoided in this fallen world. God will see you through the floods and fires of ministry life. He will even use them for his purposes in your life, whether to grow you or to teach you. Either way, the Lord will see you safely through. Rest in him.

For Further Meditation

Work through Exodus 18 more thoroughly to find principles that speak to your situation right now. Then spend some time in Isaiah 43, remembering that you are serving a God who knows and loves you, saves and sustains you, and marks you with his name for his glory. Stand firm in that today!

Day 15

I Worry about My Kids

> *Jesus, however, invited them: "Let the little children come to me, and don't stop them, because the kingdom of God belongs to such as these. Truly I tell you, whoever does not receive the kingdom of God like a little child will never enter it."*
> Luke 18:16–17

"I remember the first day I sent my oldest into the school yard. He was in first grade and assigned to the "purple" class. The problem was, I didn't know what purple was in the local language. It's not a common color, so not a word I had learned. Thankfully, we got past that hurdle only to find that each day would be a challenge for him. When one child misbehaved, the whole class got punished. We had a lot of conversations, and I struggled wondering if our choice would create permanent damage. Every decision about schooling increases my stress."

"I thought getting away from our secular culture would be a good thing for my kids, but now they seem to be facing a whole new set of issues. Am I messing up my kids by living in another country or serving full-time in ministry? How will our choices affect them in the future?"

Help Me, Lord!

God loves your children.

Do you think God didn't take into consideration that his call on your life would affect others? The family unit is his creation after all, and there are multiple examples of families in Scripture, including many with issues. Just as church life is messy, so is family; and no matter where we live, and no matter how much we shelter and teach our children, they are going to face trials in life. Who doesn't know a pastor's kid who went astray or a homeschooler who rebelled?

The problem isn't our ministry choices, but rather the fallen world in which we live. As much as God loves your children, so too does Satan seek to attack them because you've chosen to put your life—and by extension, theirs—in God's hands. So the issue isn't about ministry but about your choice of lords. God created the family as an expression of his relationship in Trinity. Satan works against the family because doing so attacks the essence of God.

Anxiety is anti-trust.

When we fail to entrust our children into God's hands, worry and anxiety eat at our minds, bodies, and spiritual life. Not only does the Lord know we're not trusting him, but our children do as well. Our words, actions, and facial expressions betray us. Our anxiety makes them anxious, because we're conveying to them that the God we follow is not in control, can't take care of this issue, or is out of touch.

When worry and fear weigh heavy, meditate on the words of Scripture:

> *Anxiety in a person's heart weighs it down, but a good word cheers it up.* (Prov 12:25)

> *Don't worry about anything, but in everything, through prayer and petition with thanksgiving, present your requests to God.* (Phil 4:6)

> *For God has not given us a spirit of fear, but one of power, love, and sound judgment.* (2 Tim 1:7)

> *Don't let your heart be troubled. Believe in God; believe also in me.* (John 14:1)

> *Can any of you add one moment to his life span by worrying?* (Matt 6:27)

As you think about what these verses communicate, remember that the last two were spoken by our Lord Jesus himself. He's telling us not to let our hearts be troubled—instead, believe in him. That includes believing in him *for our children.* He then adds a word about worry. It doesn't accomplish anything! Choose to trust.

Give your children to God in prayer.

For us, as parents, children can be a point of weakness in our faith if we are not constantly laying them before the throne of God in prayer. Too often that's why we don't even know what to pray for our children. Our love for them blinds us to what God's will is for their lives. Thankfully, we have the Spirit to help us. In our weakness, the Spirit intercedes for us (Rom 8:26).

One thing we can pray for our children is that they would always be aware of how the Lord is working out his good purposes in their lives. Our goal as parents is no different from any other area of our lives—to seek first God's kingdom and righteousness (Matt 6:33–34). That doesn't mean this world is without trouble; we're already aware of that. But it does mean that as a family we rest in God's sovereignty over all.

Jesus also reminds us in this section of the Sermon on the Mount (Matt 6:25–34) that we need to face each issue with our children on a day-by-day basis. Worrying about things that haven't yet happened gets us nowhere. Let tomorrow worry about itself. Today has enough trouble. Satan loves to get us to project into the future, especially into a future that will have a negative impact on our children. Don't go there. Nip worry in the bud.

Talk with your children about your struggles.

As parents, we're typically afraid of appearing weak and uncertain before our children. However, by being transparent with them, they can learn more about what it means to grow in their own faith. When problems come up with the language, the culture, or their school, confess to them that you don't know what's best, but you know who does. Praying together in the midst of your uncertainty opens the door for God to reveal his will and way to each one of you.

We can also talk with our children about how God can use a specific trial for his glory and their growth. Talk about how God is teaching you through this, and encourage them to see ways that he might be teaching them too.

For Further Meditation

Go back through the Scriptures about worry and anxiety in this devotion. Make a list of all the things you've been worrying about related to your children. Discuss this list with your spouse, and then pray together, confessing each issue to the Lord. Then, if appropriate, pray through the list as a family, asking God to reveal how he wants each of you to work through these issues.

Day 16

I Don't See Any Fruit

*I planted, Apollos watered, but God gave the growth.
So, then, neither the one who plants nor the one who
waters is anything, but only God who gives the growth.*
1 Corinthians 3:6–7

"When I first arrived on the field, I thought I would write to my supporters and prayer warriors every week or at least once a month. Everything was new and exciting. Now, I've got nothing! My last letter was six months ago, because there is nothing new in my life. There's certainly no ministry yet. I'm finished with language school, but I still don't have enough proficiency to do what I was called here to accomplish—and I'm embarrassed. My national partner is not helping, and I don't even see my teammates."

"I got an email from friends who went through orientation with me and are serving in another region. They were praising the Lord for all the people they've seen come to faith since they started serving. God is obviously doing great things there, and I'm happy for them. I'm just not sure why they're seeing fruit and I'm not. I'm working just as hard and using the same methods of evangelism. Am I doing something wrong? Maybe I shouldn't be here."

"I have nothing to write in my newsletters because there is no fruit. I don't think my supporters want to hear about my struggles with the language, the culture, and life in general. I don't think they want to hear about how hard it is to find opportunities to share. I'm trying to live out my faith and share the gospel, but it's not making a dent in the lives of these people."

Help Me, Lord!

Should the harvest never come.

I heard a Bill and Gloria Gaither song before I left for my first short-term mission. I couldn't decide at the time if it was supposed to encourage or discourage me, but the words have stuck with me in over thirty years of service.

> Should the harvest never come, I still will praise you.
> Should I not tie the sheaves with my own hand.
> I still will praise you for the promise of the sowing,
> And though I should never see it,
> I know the harvest will be grand.[1]

Other verses in the song say that even if the harvest never comes, we should not doubt but work with joy. We will choose to praise the Lord, who is the Lord of the harvest.

Our role in the harvest.

Even though we know what Scripture says about being seed-sowers, it is hard not being among those who are reaping what has been sowed among the lost and dying. After seeing a harvest with an unlikely woman while he waited at Jacob's well, just outside a town in Samaria, Jesus had a few words to say about harvesting.

> "My food is to do the will of him who sent me and to finish his work," Jesus told them. "Don't you say, 'There are still four more months, and then comes the harvest'? Listen to what I'm telling you: Open your eyes and look at the fields, because they are ready for harvest. The reaper is already receiving pay and gathering fruit for eternal life, so that the sower and reaper can rejoice together. For in this case the saying is true: 'One sows and another reaps.' I sent you to reap what you didn't labor for; others have labored, and you have benefited from their labor." (John 4:34–38)

We can learn several things from this story.

---

[1] William J. Gaither. Lyricist: Gloria Gaither. "Should the Harvest Never Come." 1984. Capitol CMG.

- Jesus is the Lord of the harvest. He came for a specific purpose and reaped a great harvest to prepare the way for his work of atonement through the cross and resurrection. We cannot compare our circumstances to his. He is truly the master in this area.
- The work of the gospel is a process. Some prepare the ground, others spread the seeds, and others reap the harvest. At times, we represent any one of these three in the process, and it takes discernment and prayer to identify and be at peace with our part.
- Your role in the harvest right now is a reason to rejoice. You may not see any fruit after much labor, sweat, and struggle in the field, but that doesn't mean the harvest isn't coming. What does God say to each of his servants who put their "talents" to work? "Well done, good and faithful servant!" (Matt 25:14–16, 21). Be faithful and be glad to be a part of what he's doing in the lives of each person you impact for the kingdom.

Even one who comes to faith is a harvest.

When I think about the individuals who came to faith through our ministry, I relate them to Isaiah 41:17–20. The Lord, through his prophet Isaiah, speaks of changing barren lands into fertile places, with pools of water. In the wilderness, he will plant trees not commonly found in such isolated terrain.

The reason this passage speaks to me is because in many cases, during my years of service, those who came to faith lived in hard places, were without much fellowship, and faced attacks and persecution. They are like trees in the wilderness to me, *but* they are still trees—fruit provided by God. Sometimes, the testimony of one new believer can give a powerful witness to "the hand of the LORD" (v. 20) being in this place.

Another prophet tells us not to despise "the day of small things" (Zech 4:10). Don't be disappointed with just one coming to faith, one being willing to listen to a Bible story, or one who says they will think about what you've said. This is not a contest but a journey in obedience to the call of God to go and make disciples.

Remember those who've gone before.

You are not alone in your anguish over a lack of fruit. Reading biographies of others who have served over the centuries helps regain perspective. Some showed no fruit, but remained faithful. Their working of the soil in that specific place of service brought amazing harvests in later years.

Their lives also inspired future generations to pursue God's call and bring harvests in completely different areas. All of that is fruit, so don't discount the seemingly "small impact" you're having for the kingdom.

For Further Meditation

Listen to Bill and Gloria Gaither's song and let the words speak to your heart, then meditate on the words of Jesus and Paul in relation to the harvest fields. Ask God to show you your role in the work of the fields and choose to rejoice despite the struggles.

Day 17

Why Is There So Much Evil?

> Many are asking, "Who can show us anything good?"
> Psalm 4:6a

"I was shocked. I'm here to serve refugees, and it's hard! I don't know the language of my host country, so when I use the language of the refugees I serve, the locals don't like it. After a recent influx of new refugees, attacks against them ramped up, and I found just serving them to be unsafe. The locals don't like the fact that outside aid and food distribution goes to the refugees when they are suffering too. People can be so cruel; I've been yelled at more than once just for helping refugees. The refugees are unhappy and living in horrible conditions, because no one wants to help anymore. A short-term crisis has turned into years."

"I walk by the shrines and temples in my city and instantly feel the oppression. People spend crazy amounts of money and time trying to appease their gods. Fear drives everything. That same fear keeps people from being open to the good news of Christ."

"I feel the darkness all around me. This country is so bleak; the people never smile. Hatred and revenge seem to be the only recourse people turn to in times of trouble. I've never seen so much evil in one place. I feel it affecting me, my marriage, and even my children."

Help Me, Lord!

Why Is There So Much Evil?

Don't forget what Jesus told us.

Suffering is a given in this world. Even so, we can have courage, because he has overcome the world (John 16:33 NIV). Evil is everywhere. We see it most clearly in places which are not home turf to us, because everything is new to our eyes—whereas at home we've grown up with the contrasts and are complacent to the wrongs perpetrated for the sake of evil. The presence of evil appears more evident because in most cultures there is no Judeo-Christian foundation of laws and moral values to push back against it. People accept bad things as fate, while doing nothing to right the wrong.

Evil has been in the world since that first sad day back in the garden. Jesus makes no excuses for it: "You will have suffering in this world" (John 16:33). It's a fact, a reality, an ever-present danger. Those without Christ feel its impact daily, but for those in Christ, including you, there is peace, breathing space, and room for hope. In fact, this is what we are here to share with others: our good news that, in Christ, evil does not have the upper hand. Evil has an expiration date!

When you see nothing good, remember.

Our verse for this devotion comes from Psalm 4, a psalm of David. It's another reminder that God is open to our questions, our hurts, and our cries for help. When I read the word *selah* in the Psalms, I always think of a sigh. I think it works very well with the focus of this psalm. Read Psalm 4. Notice the middle portion of this psalm. There are two imperatives for us to follow: know and reflect, and in between—don't sin in your anger.

What do we know? We know that the Lord has set us apart for himself. He has given us purpose and a call to fulfill. He's listening and will answer as you call out to him, but just remember that you are doing it as his child, his chosen one, his ambassador.

We also are told to reflect. Take your anger at evil and think about it in a calm, restful way. When we're agitated over evil, we do or think things that go against God's Word and way. Don't do that. God understands and allows us to be angry, but without sin. Maybe that's why it's important to be silent about it. Our mouths can get us in trouble!

Continue to offer yourself as the living sacrifice God has called you to be (Rom 12:1) and trust him to take care of evil. When people ask you,

"Who can show us anything good?" let them see the light of Christ in your face and through your words and actions. Remember that in him we have joy despite the darkness, and rest and sleep in the midst of trials. In Christ we have safety.

Give as you have received.

As you reflect on what you've received from God through Christ, another psalm of David helps us when evil threatens to overwhelm. Read Psalm 12 and see the response that the Lord, through David, gives to the one who finds no one faithful or loyal to the Lord.

Are you comforted by these words? They are brutally honest, yet full of hope. Think about how blessed you are as a follower of Christ to have such words to read in times of struggle, then think about the people around you who don't. This is the reason most don't smile and feel left without recourse when sin abounds.

Start with these words of complaint when God opens a door with a person. Ask them if it feels like there are no faithful people in their lives or country or if loyalty is unknown. Most will say yes and join you in despair at the evil that seems rampant. Once you're there, you have another open door—to share the good news that God will have his day, and evil does not win in the end. In the meantime, they can know peace and find value in life, while worthless things are exalted by others. All this is available in Christ.

Recognizing evil has its purposes.

The more evil raises its ugly head and Satan plays his cards openly in our world, the more opportunities we have to show the difference Christ makes in our lives. The trials Jesus spoke about will continue to increase as his return draws near, causing the love of many to grow cold (Matt 24:12–14).

As evil increases, we must guard our hearts against our love growing cold. Instead, recognize that in the midst of the darkness, our lights for Christ shine even brighter. This is our time to live in contrast to the lawless, hateful mindset—and as we do, to share about the one who enables us to stand firm.

For Further Meditation

Reflect on Jesus's actions and words in the final days of his life on earth, knowing the evil intent of men was coming to a head and the cross was the goal. Think about how a perfect, innocent man faced such evil. Did he turn inward, pull away, or shirk his purpose? No, he pressed on, taught his disciples till the end, faced accusations without retort, and willingly submitted himself to the cross. The ultimate evil was committed against the spotless, perfect lamb that we might stand firm till he returns. Talk with colleagues or family about your struggles with the evil that surrounds you. Pray together for comfort and strength.

Day 18

I Miss My Mom

> *Listen, my son, to your father's instruction,*
> *and don't reject your mother's teaching.*
> Proverbs 1:8

"I talk to my mom every day—or I did talk with her every day until we moved overseas. Now the time difference gets in the way, and either I forget or she calls and wakes me up. It's just not the same. She hasn't visited yet and can't visualize what I'm telling her, even though I've sent pictures. I struggle because I can't tell her everything; if I did, she'd just worry, and I don't want her to do that. There have never been any secrets between us, but now there has to be, even if just to protect her. Apparently she's keeping things from me too, because my sister had to tell me that Mom went to the doctor. She pretends everything is alright, but I know better."

"I'm really struggling with my teenager, and I think I've started menopause. My emotions are all over the place, and I so miss my mom right now. She's been gone for several years now, and I miss being able to call her for help. She would understand all this, but she's not here."

"I know I shouldn't complain. I know that I can still call my mom and Facetime her. The world is much smaller than it used to be. As much as I know all that, I still miss my mom! I didn't even know she'd been sick until after the fact, and I know she's missing me too. I'm not sure I could handle it if something happened to her."

Help Me, Lord!

Jesus understands.

I think that's one of the great benefits of the Incarnation—confidence that Jesus understands our feelings and struggles. Here he was, God in the flesh, and yet he spent thirty years under the care of a woman who was like the rest of us. Jesus had a mother. He was mothered, loved, fed, cared for, and let go. When I think about missing my mother, I think more about how much Mary missed Jesus. I cannot imagine how hard it was for her to let him out of her sight, knowing that all he said and did was toward one purpose—the redemption of mankind. I'm sure my mother missed me when I moved thousands of miles away, not once but twice; but Mary would have felt the pain in a much different way.

And Jesus—would he have missed his mother? I believe he did. As the God of all love and compassion, I am sure he had developed a unique bond with the woman who devoted her life to his care. Not only that, but he left home when his mother was a widow, Joseph having died at an earlier time. I'm sure he felt responsible for her. In fact, I know he did, because this was on his mind in the last moments of his life:

> Standing by the cross of Jesus were his mother, his mother's sister, Mary the wife of Clopas, and Mary Magdalene. When Jesus saw his mother and the disciple he loved standing there, he said to his mother, "Woman, here is your son." Then he said to the disciple, "Here is your mother." And from that hour the disciple took her into his home. (John 19:25–27)

Only then does Scripture tell us that Jesus knew that everything was now finished. Provision for his mother was the final act before touching his lips to the sponge full of sour wine and giving up his spirit (John 19:28–30).

Give your mother reason to rejoice.

In our pain of loss and separation, we can show our love for our mothers. The Proverbs tell us to let our mothers rejoice (Prov 23:25). Mothers love to be proud of their children. Sometimes they are proud of us even when we are less than excellent, like when playing sports or in our academic studies. However, as we serve Christ, we can also bring great joy to our mothers, especially to those who are also our sisters in the faith.

Mothers make the greatest prayer warriors, because they are already naturally on their knees for their children. Don't let her miss being a part of what God is teaching you and doing in and through you and others as you serve. Let her be one of the first to hear your requests for prayer.

There is no greater joy for a mother than to see her children walking in the truth and being faithful in service for the kingdom. Engaging her in the process will draw you closer together and be a blessing to both of you.

Adult children must learn to leave and cleave.

Even as Scripture uses marriage as an example of how a child must leave his parents to cleave to his wife, so too do we as adults need to learn to leave our parents to cleave to the Lord. The relationship between a mother and her child is precious, but just as a mother bird must encourage her children to leave the nest and fly on their own, so too are we to learn to fly forward in the path of Christ and not be hindered by an unhealthy desire to remain close to our mothers.

Jesus's words can be hard to hear on this subject, but they are his words, and they are intended for those who claim to follow him. He made clear to his disciples that families would be divided because of him, turning even a daughter against her mother. Jesus said we are not worthy of him if we love our parents more than our Lord (Matt 10:34–39).

Are you willing to offer up your relationship with your mother to the Lord? Ask if your longing for your mother is getting in the way of your longing for Christ and your service to him. How can you build a healthy relationship with your mother that will honor God?

God uses older women.

Paul's letter to Titus is so encouraging and reminds us that the Lord can use older women in our lives when our mothers are gone or live across the ocean (Titus 2:3–4). When I was a single young woman in my first place of service, God blessed me with a colleague who had children near my age. She actually had the same birthday as my mother and willingly became my adopted mom. If you're struggling with missing your mom, find a woman who can be your source of wisdom and support.

For Further Meditation

The entire tenth chapter of Matthew is worthy of study and reflection. As one commissioned by Christ for ministry, what do his words in Matthew 10 say to you? Are they too hard to hear? Why?

Tell God what's causing you distress over separation from your mother, and let his Spirit speak, bringing to light any sin that needs confessing or wrongs made right. Then, speak to your mother about your struggles, too, asking her to pray with you through them.

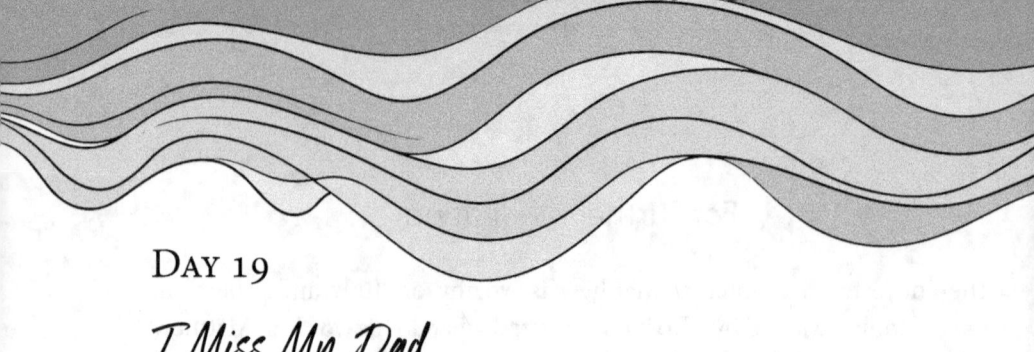

Day 19

I Miss My Dad

> *A father to the fatherless, a defender of widows,*
> *is God in his holy dwelling.*
> *God sets the lonely in families.*
> Psalm 68:5–6a (NIV)

"I'm a Daddy's girl. Hate to admit it, but true. As the youngest of my siblings, I had a special bond with my father. When everyone else had left home, he still had me to talk with, and concentrated time together drew us closer. We could talk about anything. I miss our deep discussions about God's Word and the church. Because I went to seminary, he loved talking with me about the Bible and theology. He visited me on the field more than once. None of my other siblings had such a close relationship. Now he's gone, and I have lost my best friend and biggest supporter."

"I miss my dad. His health isn't great, and I'm so sad that he can't come for a visit to see all that God's doing here and in my life. My dad could fix anything. Mom always relied on him to take care of anything that broke in our house. I wish he could come and fix stuff in mine. I'm handy, but nothing like him. With his hearing loss, it's hard to talk over the phone."

"I really need my dad right now. He could solve this issue in the house or answer my questions. I miss his wisdom. He was so good at leading in our home, and I'm struggling. I feel like such a failure at this adulting thing! I could always rest just knowing he was around."

Help Me, Lord!

I Miss My Dad

Jesus was separated from his dad too.

When I think about the cost Christ paid to come to this earth, the thing that must have been the hardest was loss of that intimate relationship with his Father. Confined to the body of an earthly man, gone were the days of perfect harmony in relationship with the Father and the Spirit. He was limited and cut off, and the devil chose to make the most of that situation, tempting him at his lowest point in the wilderness. Still, Jesus had a comeback that works for us as well:

> *Then Jesus was led up by the Spirit into the wilderness to be tempted by the devil. After he had fasted forty days and forty nights, he was hungry. Then the tempter approached him and said, "If you are the Son of God, tell these stones to become bread." He answered, "It is written: Man must not live on bread alone but on every word that comes from the mouth of God."* (Matt 4:1–4)

Everything he had learned from the Father he carried with him to earth. Of course, we don't have the unlimited knowledge of God the Father that Jesus had, but we do have the Word of God to help us in our walk of faith; and we also have the wisdom of our earthly fathers to guide us. When you are missing your dad, think about the things he said, what he taught you, or how he lived. Thank the Lord for what you learned and seek to live by it.

Strive to bring honor to your father.

What makes a father the happiest? Seeing his children grow into independent, godly men and women. As a parent, I've often said, "My children are much better than I was." This holds true for many fathers as they watch their sons and daughters surpass their own achievements and dreams. Proverbs 23:24 states that righteous and wise sons know the blessing of their fathers rejoicing and delighting in them.

What is more important, to always be close to and dependent on your father or to bring him honor and joy by serving God to your best? Remember, in honoring your parents, you honor God. In honoring our parents, God blesses our lives (Exod 20:12).

Honoring our parents reveals our obedience to God's desires. When we obey, he blesses. Be encouraged that your work for the Lord brings such honor (Deut 5:16 and Eph 6:2).

It is difficult when your father is facing illness and you long to be near him. There are times when we are able to take leave and minister to a parent, but if you're struggling because you're not able to leave your place of ministry, seek ways to honor your father even while separated. What can you do to help your siblings better serve him? How can you bless your sibling or mother for the extra work they're facing because you're not there? What encouragement can you give to your father? Ask about his health and needs, but also make sure he's hearing about all that God is doing in your life and in the lives of the people you serve.

God is the Father of all fathers.

Just as Christ is King of kings and Lord of lords, God Almighty is Father of fathers. If your earthly father is no longer in your life or has passed away, Psalm 68:5–6a reminds us that God is the father of the fatherless. I chose to use the New International Version for the Scripture presented at the beginning of this Day 19 because I love this phrase: "God sets the lonely in families."

While we have a heavenly Father who watches over us, teaches us, and guides us, God has also set us into families where we have access to men who serve as examples for us. Whether you marry into a family with a godly father who takes you under his wing, or an older man in the church or on your mission team serves in that role, in your longing for your father, don't forget to look to those he has provided for you at just such a time. Your faithful Father cares for you.

For Further Meditation

Think about the relationship of Jesus with God the Father. What lessons can you take from what he modeled for us here on earth? Even his cry on the cross shows the agony of the separation caused by the sin of man, and he did cry out. Maybe that is what you need to do today. Let the Lord hear your struggle, then also let the loving arms of your heavenly Father bring you peace. Live in such a way as to honor both your heavenly Father and your earthly fathers.

Day 20

I Can't Believe What I'm Accused of, Lord

*They surround me with hateful words
and attack me without cause.*
Psalm 109:3

"We have ten days to leave the country. My wife is five months pregnant with our first child. We stood before the officer to hear the verdict, and she lost it; her hormones raged. He accused us of being a threat to national security, and she questioned how she could be a threat in her condition. I don't think he meant *her*, but she took it personally. Yes, I've been discipling people who had come to faith from the majority religion, but no one was coerced to faith. Besides, there aren't that many, so how could it trigger such a threat? It reminds me of our friends who were kicked out earlier this year in retaliation for a crackdown on fundamentalists. Is there no justice?"

"I don't see anything that can prove that I've broken any laws. I heard that someone in the church is accusing me of preaching falsehood or paying people to become Christian. I can't believe the things they are accusing me of! I wonder if I should get a lawyer to fight this. While my wife cries, I can't find any words to respond. I don't think they'd do any good. How is this going to affect the rest of our team?"

Help Me, Lord!

I Can't Believe What I'm Accused of, Lord

You're not the first to be falsely accused.

Scripture is not lacking for examples of those who were falsely accused or charged. My first thought is of how Joseph—dreamer though he was—by the time he had served in the house of Potiphar, had proven himself a humbler man and served with integrity. That, however, did not stop Potiphar's wife from pursuing him and then accusing him of taking advantage of her. We know what happened to him—a jail cell. Talk about a bum rap!

Mordecai is another example. Hated only because he was of another nationality and religion. Sound familiar? Haman plotted to have not only him but all the Jewish people killed, simply because Mordecai refused to bow and give him honor. He would have succeeded too, had it not been for Queen Esther taking a risk for her people.

What do we know of the charges against Jesus? In John 15, Jesus spoke to his disciples about the charges that would soon be levied against him. He made it clear that because the world (and more specifically, the religious leaders) hated him, they too would be hated. The persecution he would face would also be directed at them. Ultimately, the hate for Christ and his current and future disciples would be without cause: "They hated me for no reason" (John 15:25).

Fight or Flight?

When accusations come, the decision either to fight or flee may seem like your only two options, but they are not. The first decision must be this: turn to God.

> *The LORD is my light and my salvation—*
> *whom should I fear?*
> *The Lord is the stronghold of my life—*
> *whom should I dread?* (Ps 27:1)

When Daniel faced attack, he went home and prayed (Dan 6). His routine of relationship with God was not altered, and this is a good example to follow. Satan desires to shake us and our faith when troubles come. Don't let him. Find your refuge in the stronghold of your relationship with God.

As you turn your face to the Lord, remember that he is not taken by surprise by these accusations. In the case of Mordecai, he used a horrible situation to save the Jews from a vengeful authority. In the case of Joseph, he used a season in prison to open the door to the salvation of his family—and his budding nation—from famine. And ultimately, in the case of Christ, his submission to false judgment paved the way for the atonement.

The accusations you face may be a way God is opening the door for the gospel to be spread to authorities or peoples who have yet to hear. He may be using them to move you to a new location where hearts are waiting for the message. The Lord might want to use this situation to humble and teach you, preparing you for something even greater. Yield to his insight and will.

Let your integrity have the final word.

False accusations can sour every aspect of your life and work. It's hard to see, in the moment, how your reputation, not to mention your witness, will ever survive. When the actions of my husband and I were questioned through a letter written to our sending organization, we were shocked. No one had come directly to us about the issues in question. Instead, they chose to write to our leadership, which had no firsthand knowledge of what we were dealing with on the field.

We chose not to retaliate but to let the integrity of our actions speak for themselves. We left the country and transferred to a place that had no established church but was ripe for harvest. Though we'd been hurt, we looked forward, choosing to keep bitterness from invading our minds and hearts. God blessed in those years after the trial, so we did not question the *why* of the actions. Though it was a hard season, we wanted God to be our defender, and he proved faithful.

> *Vindicate me, LORD,*
> *because I have lived with integrity*
> *and have trusted in the Lord without wavering.* (Ps 26:1)

If you have acted in faith and integrity of mind and heart, then rest. Rest in knowing that God is in control even if you don't understand why this is happening in your life. Let your integrity speak for itself.

For Further Meditation

Read and meditate on Psalms 26 and 27. In your struggle, lean on the Lord. Pray for your accusers, asking God to soften your heart to understand their motivations, which could be out of jealousy, a misguided faith, or the lack of a relationship with God through Christ. Remember Christ's words on the cross for those who mocked, tortured, and killed him: "Father, forgive them, because they do not know what they are doing" (Luke 23:34). Ask for the Spirit's strength to pray the same.

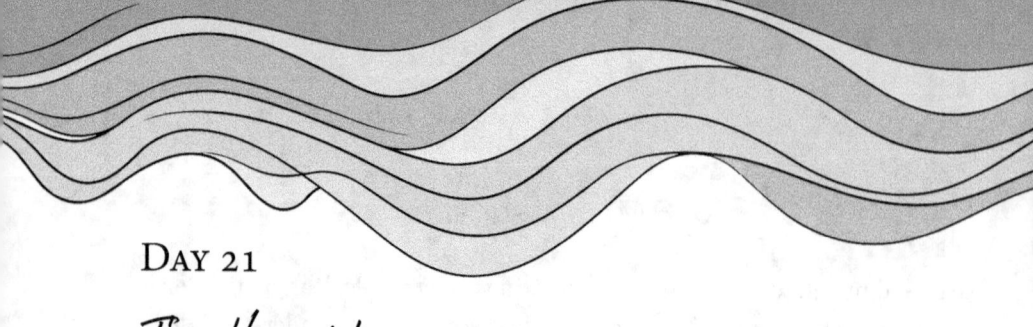

Day 21

I'm Homesick

> "Truly I tell you," Jesus said, "there is no one who has left house or brothers or sisters or mother or father or children or fields for my sake and for the sake of the gospel, who will not receive a hundred times more, now at this time—houses, brothers and sisters, mothers and children, and fields, with persecutions—and eternal life in the age to come.
> Mark 10:29–30

"My brother got married last week. I haven't been here long enough to get leave, so I missed it. My parents were so sad about my absence. My brother really wanted me to perform the ceremony, but he had to settle for his fiancée's pastor. I thought I was doing really good in this place until that happened. Somehow it really bummed me out, and I wanted to go home. I'm frustrated with language and so tired of this heat and humidity. I could be home right now!"

"When a war started in a neighboring country, I stopped functioning. And my mother, consumed with worry, was calling every day and recounting every scary piece of news she'd heard within the last twenty-four hours. I hated how I was reacting to the situation. I couldn't concentrate on ministry or language learning, as I constantly checked updates on my newsfeed. This place wasn't safe, even though my teammates told me otherwise. What did I want to do? Go home. I realized I'd had this feeling for a while, but refused to address it."

"The seasons are changing at home, but not in this place. I'm so tired of days of the same—all hot or all cold, all wet or all dry. Where are the trees and leaves, the green grass and the flowers? Our house wasn't much, but it was ours. We knew our neighbors, had great schools, and were close enough to family to visit anytime we wanted. I'm drowning in homesickness! I want to go home!"

Help Me, Lord!

I'm Homesick

Don't let an idea of home become your idol.

God's Word is clear that anything we put before our devotion to God is an idol. The last section of Luke 9 recounts the conversations Jesus had with three men who wanted to follow him, but home and family had a bit too much pull on their lives.

The first man told Jesus that he would follow him wherever he went. Jesus replied by letting the man know that Jesus himself had no home—not even a "place to lay his head" (Luke 9:58). That must have made the man think twice.

Jesus called the second man to "follow me." His reply was in the affirmative with one caveat: "First let me go bury my father" (Luke 9:59b). In Jesus's view, the spread of the good news had priority over family obligations.

The third man also wanted to follow Christ, once he told his family good-bye. Jesus asserted that there is no looking back for those called to serve the kingdom of God.

You wouldn't be reading this devotional if you hadn't already surrendered your life to kingdom service, so I have no question about your call. The second and third men, who first wanted to go back to their families, were obviously struggling with the source of their allegiance. When Jesus called Peter, he dropped his nets and followed Jesus (Luke 5:11); there was no other *first* in his life, and Peter was a married man.

Take time to talk to the Father about your homesickness. Open your heart to his searching Spirit to make sure there is no other *first* in your life.

Conquering homesickness requires forward thinking.

Moving forward in response to the call of God results in a separation from that which we cannot take with us to the field—including our home, our extended family, our home church, and so much more. Homesickness is a natural reaction to leaving. It's a kind of grief process that we all experience. The essential thing to remember is that we can't make a home in our homesickness. A heart that is looking back is not present in the moment or looking forward to the wonderful things God is doing in your midst.

> *Do not remember the past events;*
> *pay no attention to things of old.*

> *Look, I am about to do something new;*
> *Even now it is coming. Do you not see it?*
> *Indeed, I will make a way in the wilderness,*
> *rivers in the desert.* (Isa 43:18–19)

So many times in Scripture the Lord was trying to get his people to move forward, but they kept looking back. How quickly did they long for the food of Egypt after a short time in the desert (Exod 16)? Somehow they forgot that they ate it under the bondage of slavery, but that didn't stop their longing for the home they knew.

Those moved into exile in Babylon for a refining by the Lord are encouraged through the prophet Jeremiah to settle there and make a home (Jer 29:1–14). The Lord at times moves us from one place of service to another for reasons we can't understand in the moment, yet even in such times he wants us to look forward, not backward. We lived in six countries in our twenty years of service, and I constantly had to turn to this passage as a reminder to let my heart and mind settle, whether I wanted to be there or not.

Home is where the heart is.

A heart longing for something left behind is not longing for God. The longer I live on this earth, the more I realize that this earth is not my home. Going back to what we thought we knew is not the answer to our problems. Many who have returned realize that home is not the same—they've changed, and thus the way they see home changes. It no longer satisfies the longing. When we realize that home is where God is, then all desires for earthly homes fade. They don't go away, of course, because God meant for us to live in the confines of a family and home, but they no longer hold as much sway over our lives. His will and purposes take precedent.

> *Happy are the people whose strength is in you,*
> *whose hearts are set on pilgrimage.* (Ps 84:5)

Remembering that this life is a journey, a pilgrimage in service to the glory of God, helps us rest in the seasons of change and service, wherever they might take us. When Jesus was speaking to his disciples just prior to his suffering and death, he shared this:

> *If anyone loves me, he will keep my word. My Father will love him, and we will come to him and make our home with him.* (John 14:23)

In Christ, our heart is his home. Our desire should be that he is settled in us more than we are settled in this world. When we've given him free reign to take up residence in our heart, then the location of our earthly residence will be of no consequence.

For Further Meditation

In your struggle, pray through Psalm 6. It's OK to be hurting and missing home—just make sure you're talking to the Lord about it. As he calms your heart, through the work of the Holy Spirit, turn to Psalm 84, and look forward with anticipation to how he will teach and use you in this new season and place. Do all this with a thankful heart.

Day 22

I Hate This Place

I am not praying that you take them out of the world but that you protect them from the evil one.
John 17:15

"I haven't left our apartment for over a week. I let my husband go out to get groceries or take the kids to school. I have no desire to get outside of this flat. Thankfully, my husband is happy to pick up the slack, because, after all, he's the one who really has a love for this place and the people we're supposed to be serving. I'm not there yet. I answered the call with him, but I didn't realize until I saw where we were living that it really wasn't mine in the first place."

"A guy made me feel like an idiot today. I was sharing the gospel, and he started making fun of my accent. Needless to say, he didn't hear the rest of the story. I just said, 'Never mind,' and left. My ministry partner told me to shrug it off, but I can't. This is just one of many irritating things that have happened lately to discourage me. I just can't seem to get a break with the people. They are so self-satisfied in their secular lives."

"I'm miserable. This place is nothing like I imagined it would be. I've never seen so much filth, and the electricity goes off way too much. I thought it would be like an adventure, but the day-in-day-out effort it takes just to survive is too much for me. I hate this place! I can't live here any longer!"

Help Me, Lord!

Jesus left a palace for a manger.

If there is anything in Scripture that makes us stop in our tracks regarding complaining, it's a reminder of the price Jesus paid to live among us. I know it might not be what you want to hear right now, but since Jesus was never one to beat around the bush, I don't think we should in facing the reality of this complaint. Paul's letter to the believers in Philippi made clear that we should "do nothing out of selfish ambition or conceit" (Phil 2:3). We need to be putting the interests of others before our own by adopting the same attitude as Christ Jesus, our Lord.

The salvation we gain through the sacrifice of Christ should lead us to sacrifice the comforts of this world that others might know him. If God has called you to this place, he must have a reason. Perhaps he sees in you the ability to handle adversity with grace for the cause of Christ. He might have called you here to stretch your faith, leading you to go to a deeper level of trust so you can give testimony to others of his faithfulness. He could have brought you to such a place to free you from the worries of the material world and give you a renewed understanding of his purposes.

Whatever the reason, you're in this moment of crisis because he needs to speak to you. Will you listen?

There was nothing good about Nineveh to Jonah.

If there is a person you can possibly relate to in this moment, it's Jonah. He was a believer and committed follower of God. He was probably even a great evangelist and prophet. God obviously called him to Nineveh because he was the man for the job. The problem was, it wasn't a job Jonah wanted.

You, however, didn't have that same attitude. You answered God's call to this place and people. They are as lost as the Ninevites and maybe as wicked too, but in either case, you didn't run away; you were spared the extra trial of being swallowed by a big fish. Your realization of God's *mistake* in calling you didn't happen until after you entered the city gates. Now you're here and you're miserable.

Yet God didn't let Jonah off the hook of his call, and I have a feeling he won't let you off the hook either. Jonah was the first prophet sent to a heathen nation, but he wasn't the last. When a place is in such sad repair, it's a reflection of the hearts of its inhabitants. Can you see beyond your living conditions to the heart condition of the people who have lived their entire lives in this place?

Commit to a change of heart.

Jonah had three days in the belly of a big fish to reflect on his situation. I don't know how long it will take with you, but perhaps reading Jonah 2:2–9 will help. Cry out to the Lord from the depths of your "Sheol" (v. 2). Jonah knew that people who cherished worthless idols abandoned their love for God. He didn't want to be like that and committed to fulfil his vow. Ask yourself if your desire for your previous life is just such a worthless idol in the eyes of the Lord.

If you are feeling your life is fading away due to your circumstances, remember the Lord and pray. No matter the attitude of the people around you, choose to offer a sacrifice of thanksgiving to the Lord your God. Fulfill your vow of obedience to his call. Move forward in obedience. That's what Jonah did.

Jonah pressed forward to the city he hated and proclaimed the message given to him by God. To his obvious surprise, the people—from the king on down—repented and turned to God. As a result, the city was spared from destruction. Jonah's willingness to be in a hard place brought amazing results.

We learn from this story that although Jonah obeyed, his heart was really not in agreement with God's plan for the people of Nineveh. God obviously set Jonah straight on that notion, reminding him that he had no right to be angry at God's sovereignty as Lord of Creation; but there is a lesson here for us as well.

Without Jesus, there is no good place to live.

When living conditions and the state of a city or country are beyond horrible in our eyes, we can easily become bitter toward the nationals. It's their fault, after all, that this place is so poorly run, corruption is rampant, and no one cares to clean things up. If we're not careful, we not only become desensitized to a place but to a people as well. This is a reminder of the reality that Jesus shared. "Because lawlessness will multiply, the love of many will grow cold" (Matt 24:12).

Rather than *lawlessness*, other versions use words like *wickedness* or *evil*, but the result is the same—cold hearts. When we are surrounded by lostness and the resulting denigration of societal structures, our hearts can grow cold toward the people, making us less willing to share the good news of Christ, which can turn everything around.

For those living in lost cultures that are centered around material wealth, the same thing happens, but believers are more like frogs in a pot of water that is slowly warming up to the point that they don't realize they've grown cold until it's too late. At least in your difficult situation, you're more acutely aware of the need for Christ. That should be some encouragement to stay put until the Lord says to move.

For Further Meditation

Begin by praying through Psalms 23 and 62. Ask the Lord to provide those green pastures and refreshing springs to help you stay the course in service. Seek the rest that only God can give through the comfort of his Spirit and his Word. Above all, pray for the people who surround you. Ask God to allow you to see them through his eyes and heart, praying for their struggles and needs.

Day 23

I Can't Afford to Keep Going

*And my God will supply all your needs
according to his riches in glory in Christ Jesus.*
Philippians 4:19

"I had no idea how hard it would be to live in this country. I had a good job back home, and now I'm dipping into my savings almost every month. I feel like I'm practically begging people for money in every one of my newsletters, and I know they get sick of hearing from me. I know how much people make in my home church. Can't they help me out? I know I should cook more at home, but I don't have time. It's just so much easier to pick something up quickly. I lived that way before, but it doesn't seem to work here."

"I don't know how much longer I can live like this. This country is much more expensive than I thought it would be, and my support level is just not meeting my needs. I'm barely making the payments on past debt and have little or no margin for the unexpected expenses that seem to pop up every month. I know God called me, but I'm not sure I can afford to keep going."

Help Me, Lord!

Will God use this to teach you about his provision?

The topic of money and financial status among the followers of God in Scripture doesn't give us the satisfaction that things are one way or the other. Think of people like Queen Esther, Joseph (when he served Pharaoh), King David, Lydia, and the Apostle Paul. These, along with Abraham, Isaac, and Jacob, all had some wealth. God used them in their business or position to fulfill his purposes. Then you had others who would have been "among the least of these" financially, like most of the prophets, apostles, and those who labored alongside Paul. They weren't rich, and many times went without food or a place to stay, but never failed in service to the kingdom.

Paul's encouragement in Philippians 4:19 (above) to the believers in Philippi can sound good, but seems to apply to others when your own bank account is overdrawn. Why is it so hard for us to serve God? Doesn't he know we need money to survive?

He knows, and yet this lesson can be a hard one. It was for the disciples, and they were living in the physical presence of the King of the Universe! They watched him feed the thousands, and yet when their stomachs growled, they couldn't focus on their rabbi's teaching about the "leaven of the Pharisees." As a result of their ignorance, he said they were "of little faith" (Matt 16:8–12).

When worries over money lead to a loss of focus.

It's easy for us to give a spiritual answer to why there was such a difference between the disciples' worries over food and money and Jesus's seemingly nonchalant attitude toward the things of this world. Of course, Jesus wouldn't worry—he was the Son of God. He could turn water into wine, multiply loaves and fishes, and live by the Word of God. The disciples, however, didn't have such abilities or even the benefit of the indwelling Spirit, at this stage, to grasp any of this. So, does that mean Jesus doesn't see or care about my needs?

Hardly. Jesus knows, and I think the main reason for the difference in our Lord's attitude toward earthly matters was that he knew his time was limited. He had three short years to soften the hearts of the Jewish people and prepare them to carry on the proclamation of the salvation he brought for generations to come. He was literally putting his physical needs into the hands of a small group of followers, so that he could focus on the urgent task at hand.

In answering the call of God to serve among the nations, you are putting your own physical needs into the hands of the body of Christ, his church, for the season he has you in this place. In trusting the church to step up to the task out of their obedience to Christ, you are then able to focus on the ministry he's given you. This requires communication and prayer. Pray first that God will put you into relationship with the people he's preparing for this important role in ministry, and then communicate with them, so they truly feel a part of the ministry. People can't give to what they don't know.

Just as we are to ask, seek, and knock through our prayers to the Lord (Matt 7:7–12), we should lay our needs out to God and to our prayer supporters. Return to your primary focus of ministry and see what God will do.

Be a steward, not a spender.

Just because a person surrenders to missions does not mean that they instantly change long-established habits related to money and spending. Spend time in prayer and ask the Lord if there is anything wrong with the way you're using the money you've been called to steward for his glory. Just as we are called to steward our time, our gifts, and our role as parents of our children, we are also to be stewards of our financial and material blessings.

Stewardship begins with giving God the firstfruits (Mal 3:10). Are you regularly setting aside a tithe to the Lord from that which you receive?

Are you diligent in your work? If you work a secular job to help provide for your family, are you serving with integrity? If you receive support from an organization or church, are you diligent in communication and wisely using those funds? Do you have accountability and live within the confines of a budget? Even if you live alone, are you keeping your spending in check? Talk with your spouse about your family's budget or get a wise friend to work with you to develop a financial plan.

How we live reflects on our witness for Christ. If I'm spending a lot in front of national friends and then complaining about a lack of funds, they will wonder why we tell them to trust our Jesus for all their needs.

My late husband often said, "Missionaries living on the same salary will either save money or always be in debt. It depends on their view of money and their stewardship or lack thereof." Be a good steward of what the Lord provides.

Even the poor can be lovers of money.

I have watched some of the very poorest of people be consumed with the desire to have money. You don't have to be rich to love money. Obviously, money was a sticky issue for the early church, as the Apostle Paul had much to say in his letters on the matter, even for leadership (1 Tim 3:1–4; 6:6–10).

We are warned to keep free from the love of money and be satisfied with what we have (Heb 13:5). Love of money will be a sign of the last days, so don't get caught up in the temptation (2 Tim 3:1–2).

For Further Meditation

Confess your needs to God, knowing he cares for you. Pray using 1 Peter 5:6–9 as your guide. Begin with humility, giving him your cares. Be alert to how Satan wants to use this time of financial trouble to disturb your faith in the loving Provider. Stand firm, and he will see you through.

Day 24

These People Don't Get It

> *Hear this,*
> *you foolish and senseless people.*
> *They have eyes, but they don't see.*
> *They have ears, but they don't hear.*
> *Do you not fear me?*
> *This is the LORD's declaration.*
> Jeremiah 5:21–22a

"I told a woman that she needed to be born again, and she replied that her first birth was enough! Wow—I couldn't believe it. There was no recognition of sin, no need for repentance, and no desire for a Savior. Later I spoke with a person about accepting Christ as Savior, and they said, 'If I accepted the Lord, then all I had suffered as a [nominal] Christian meant nothing. How could I turn my back and be disloyal to my church?'"

"I put so much time into learning their language and understanding their culture, but when I share the gospel, it seems to go right through them. It's like they aren't even listening. Don't they see how miserable their lives are without Jesus? Why don't they get it?! I feel like I'm beating my head against a wall!"

Help Me, Lord!

These People Don't Get It

God gives us Jeremiah for such times.

I have a strong affinity for the prophet Jeremiah, maybe because one of my spiritual gifts is prophecy and I feel his pain. I also feel his frustration, as God had given him the difficult task of preaching to the people of Judah, warning them about the impending doom of destruction and exile if they do not turn back to God. This was a people group who should have known better, for they knew their heritage and had the Law, but they had rejected everything to go after false gods and worthless idols. Sound familiar?

Some of us are called to serve among people groups who have no background in Christianity, while others serve where there was once a strong foundation but it has crumbled under secularism, false teaching, or nominalism. There are challenges in sharing the truth of Christ in both situations, and we can often face pushback and frustration.

As you struggle with constant roadblocks to acceptance, consider what Jeremiah faced. Some made plans to denounce him publicly and pay no attention to his words. Others called for him to be sentenced to death. Officials accused him of defecting to the Chaldeans, so had him beaten and imprisoned. Other officials lowered him into a cistern, where he sank into the mud (see Jer 18:18; 26:11; 37:14–16; 38:6).

Jeremiah had it rough. Yet—oh, how important to say *yet*—he continued to preach the word of the Lord faithfully to the people, as he'd been called.

When all you meet is opposition—pray.

Even though Jeremiah wasn't always easy on the people he was called to reach, he remained open in his communication with the Lord about them.

> *I know, LORD,*
> *that a person's way of life is not his own;*
> *no one who walks determines his own steps.*
> *Discipline me, LORD, but with justice—*
> *not in your anger,*
> *or you will reduce me to nothing.*
> *Pour out your wrath on the nations*
> *that don't recognize you*
> *and on the families*

> *that don't call on your name,*
> *for they have consumed Jacob;*
> *they have consumed him and finished him off*
> *and made his homeland desolate.* (Jer 10:23–25)

In our frustration, we must make sure our slate is clean with the Lord. Jeremiah was not afraid to ask for the Lord's discipline. We know God's judgment is coming on the nations and those who turn their backs on Christ, but we must guard our own hearts against bitterness toward others. Jeremiah wanted to make sure his heart was pure before God. Yes, wrath was coming, but he was counting on God's mercy toward him and those who believed.

Read the raw, honest prayer of the prophet in Jeremiah 18:19–23. It hits the mark at times when we are feeling pressure to throw up our hands. God knows what we are facing. Whether direct or indirect attacks, he's not blind to our struggles and pain. In Christ, however, we know that those who continue to turn against the Lord will not only dig a pit of despair in this life but will face God's final wrath on the last day.

This is why the prophet's prayer that his fellow Israelites would "be forced to stumble before" the Lord (Jer 18:23) is worthy of note. In their rejection of our message of hope, I do pray that some people will stumble in their unbelief, grow dissatisfied with their lifestyle or misguided faith, and be laid low before the truth of the gospel.

We have no reason to pray for revenge against the lost, because we know that God will have the last say in the matter, but we can pray that at some point in their lives circumstances will cause them to seek out the hope we've shared.

Remain a faithful sower until the harvest comes.

Read the parable of the sower in Matthew 13. Even Jesus knew that not all would hear and respond to his preaching in faith. This does not stop the laborer from sowing the seed. We press on in the task because, as he said, we've been blessed to see and hear (Matt 13:16), witnessing the work of Christ through the power of the Holy Spirit in our own lives and in the lives of many others. Jeremiah never got to see such things, but he faithfully preached despite the rejection. And because he did, we have the words of God for our generation, along with his example of faithfulness.

The soil of your area of service may be rocky or full of thorns; but the more you work it, removing the stones and pulling up the thorns, the more receptive the ground will be—maybe not in your day, but for the one who follows.

Guard your heart.

As you grow in your trust of the Lord in this difficult time, be humble, guard your heart against bitterness, and take time to offer up thanksgiving in the midst of your hurt. When you don't understand why, remain, like David in Psalm 131, submissive to his sovereignty.

For Further Meditation

Use the cries of Jeremiah or the psalmists to pour your heart out to the Lord. Pray for the people who are standing strong against the message of Christ. Ask the Lord to soften your heart toward them and to show you anything in your own life or attitude that is hindering his love from showing through you to them. Find an accountability partner to work with you through these struggles.

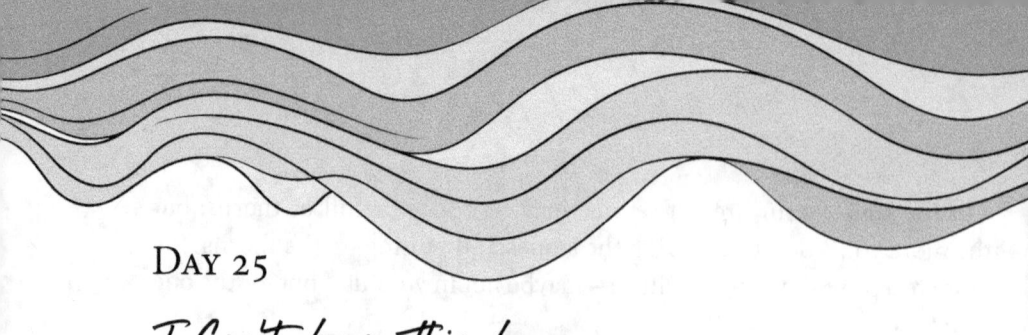

Day 25

I Can't Learn This Language

> When I came to you, brothers and sisters, announcing the mystery of God to you, I did not come with brilliance of speech or wisdom.
> 1 Corinthians 2:1

"They are sending me to a specialist. Apparently my ears aren't picking up this language. Just when I was actually beginning to do some work, I have to take a break and leave the country for this appointment. I'm not sure it will do any good, but what choice do I have? If I don't learn the language, I can't stay. I can't help but compare with my colleagues. Why would the Lord give them the ability and not me? Didn't he call me here too? What happened to God equipping us for what he calls us to do?"

"This is the hardest language in the world! Lord, why couldn't you have just sent me to an English-speaking country? Trying to make myself understood, I feel like an idiot half the time and a child most of the time. It's so humiliating! Then to understand what people are trying to tell me—it's like I've learned nothing in six months. Is this really what I'm supposed to be doing?"

Help Me, Lord!

These People Don't Get It

Even the man of multiple languages had issues.

If Paul's words meant nothing to me earlier in life, they took on so much greater meaning after I tried to learn Arabic. I had a been a French major in college, so when I went to French-speaking West Africa, I did pretty well, if I say so myself; but God brought me down several notches when it came to learning Arabic. Though I carried around my own translator, in the person of my Egyptian-American husband, I knew I would still have to learn to survive in this difficult language, which really is one of the hardest in the world.

Look at the rest of this passage from Paul's letter to the believers in Corinth. Read 1 Corinthians 2:1–5. Even Paul admits to facing them earlier in weakness, fear, and trembling. He knew his words and the way he spoke were not "persuasive words of wisdom," but yet he was not discouraged. He had something that could overcome any deficiencies—the Holy Spirit.

Paul recognized his own weakness in speech. Perhaps he had the words in Greek to communicate with the Corinthians, but having the vocabulary doesn't mean we convey the words in a way people understand. He obviously felt the disconnect, and it troubled him. At the same time, because of his own self-awareness, he was powerfully aware of the work of God through him. Sometimes it's in our weakest moments that God does his greatest work.

If we look at the verses just prior to Paul's confession of his weakness, he reveals a great truth about all who are called by Christ:

> God has chosen what is foolish in the world to shame the wise, and God has chosen what is weak in the world to shame the strong. God has chosen what is insignificant and despised in the world—what is viewed as nothing—to bring to nothing what is viewed as something, so that no one may boast in his presence. It is from him that you are in Christ Jesus, who became wisdom from God for us—our righteousness, sanctification, and redemption—in order that, as it is written: Let the one who boasts, boast in the Lord. (1 Cor 1:27–31)

Let any progress you make be from him.

When you're struggling with language, look at it as an opportunity for God to shine through you. When I arrived in Ivory Coast, a freshly minted graduate in French, I thought I knew it all. In some ways, I did have a head start. I could actually speak the language upon arrival at the airport, and thus hit the ground running. What I didn't have, even with my best French accent, was a grasp of the culture upon which I had just descended—and boy, did I blow it more than once, in perfect French and all!

For this reason, I think Paul's words resonate even more. For me, that first missions experience was one in which I thought I had arrived in strength, but soon discovered just how weak I was. It was only when I was sufficiently humbled at my own shortcomings that God was allowed to work through me. Moving, several years later, to the Middle East, I knew where I stood, and it wasn't on top or even partway up! Even with some Arabic lessons under my belt, I was not proficient and held no thought of being self-sufficient. I needed God all the way.

As I began to make progress in the language, I gave God all the credit. Any progress in this impossibly hard language was all him. How I began to make sense of words that had no relation to my native English was beyond me. I stood in awe of how he helped my brain to comprehend, and I gave him thanks. You can do the same.

Don't judge anything prematurely.

You may be in the throes of despair right now, but don't stay there. Think back on what you've learned from the first day of lessons till now. Surely there are words or phrases you didn't know that you can now speak and hear with confidence. Rejoice in that. These days are days of testing, not just of our language ability but of our trust in God and his purposes for our lives. Paul had so much to say about this to the believers in Corinth.

> *So don't judge anything prematurely, before the Lord comes, who will both bring to light what is hidden in darkness and reveal the intentions of the hearts. And then praise will come to each one from God.* (1 Cor 4:5)

Read verses 6 through 13 of that same chapter. What is God revealing about the intentions of your heart in the midst of language learning? Are you patient in his preparation of you for the task? Are you willing to humble yourself for the job of language learning so that in the days to come the people you serve will be lifted up in the knowledge of Christ? Don't be too quick to judge this season of struggle.

> LORD, hear my prayer;
> listen to my cries for mercy.
> I call on you in the day of my distress,
> for you will answer me. (Ps 86:6–7)

For Further Meditation

Dig deeper into the words of Paul to the church in Corinth, but also pour the words of Psalm 86 over your soul as a soothing balm from the Lord. He is the God who understands us in our weaknesses, allowing his only Son to experience our struggles so that we can go to him in our time of need. As you study the language, practice with locals, and make progress toward your goal, give your frustrations—and thanks—to the God who hears and cares.

Day 26

How Can I Share If It Threatens Their Lives?

> All these were approved through their faith, but they did not receive what was promised, since God had provided something better for us, so that they would not be made perfect without us.
> Hebrews 11:39–40

"This is getting too hard. My friend's entire family had to move to another city last week because of threats against his life. Now I can't even follow up and disciple him, since he's living too far from me. He told me his wife was very upset to have to leave her parents, but it's her own brother that is threatening them. As I prayed with the guys in my discipleship group, I could tell they were worried about this development. There had been rumors that the local imam was speaking out against those who leave the faith. That's every one of the guys in my small group. How can I keep them safe?"

"It's like telling someone I have the cure for cancer, but the cure will kill them! I'm really struggling with sharing Christ with these people when I know it could cost them their jobs, their homes, and even their lives. What's good about that? How will they live? Will I be responsible for each person who's scared for his life? What if someone is killed for his faith—Does that make me an accessory? Will they come after me too?"

Help Me, Lord!

How Can I Share If It Threatens Their Lives?

The devil loves to keep us immobilized by fear.

When my late husband was living in Texas, a Muslim man came to him and said he wanted to know how to be saved. As they talked, Raouf learned that because of the man's interest in Christ and his purchase of a Bible, his family had already tried to kill him three times, including cutting the breaks on his car. Raouf was concerned. If this man's family had already tried to kill him just for having a Bible, what would they do when they knew he'd accepted Christ?

He talked to the man a while longer, and basically encouraged him to "go in peace." However, though the man left in peace, Raouf was not at peace and didn't sleep all night, knowing he had failed to lead the man to Christ. As he struggled, the Lord spoke to him and helped him realize that even if the man were to live a hundred years, he would still die and go to hell. How much better for him to live even one day in Christ and die knowing his eternity was secure. The next day, Raouf led the man to Christ!

That changed everything for Raouf Ghattas; and from that point on, he never hesitated to share the good news of Jesus with anyone he met. In his thirty-plus years of ministry, only one person was actually killed for his faith. Satan is a liar and the father of lies. He wants you to think that every person you share with will be killed for their faith, but they won't. Do believers die for their faith in this world? Yes, but does every Muslim who accepts Christ get killed? No. Don't let fear keep you from sharing.

> *The fear of mankind is a snare,*
> *but the one who trusts in the LORD is protected.*
> (Prov 29:25)

Let the Holy Spirit be your guide as you pray before you share.

Knowing when to share and with whom to share takes discernment. This comes not from our own intuitions, but from the Holy Spirit; and we must rely on him when seeking opportunities to present Christ to others. Sometimes this means we wait until we are alone with a person who seems open to the gospel. Sharing in a crowd is good for general seed sowing, but not always good for bringing in the harvest. When you know a person could face troubles for coming to Christ, pray.

> *Don't worry about anything, but in everything, through prayer and petition with thanksgiving, present your requests to God. (Phil 4:6)*

Pray before you share, pray while you're sharing, and pray afterward. At all points, you're asking the Lord not only to give you the words to say, but for the Spirit to penetrate the person's heart and mind and bring to fruition the seeds you've planted. Prayer also helps us know how to bring a person to the point of decision. In most cases, after sharing the truth of who Jesus is, you ask the person if they would like to accept him as Savior. If they're not ready to make a decision, always leave the door open by encouraging them to take all they've heard to God, asking him to give them confirmation that your words are true.

Is prayer a part of your daily life, or have you forgotten the power it brings? When we fail to seek the Spirit's guidance, we lose the courage to share our faith with boldness.

God honors those who suffer for their faith.

When we have the privilege of leading a person to faith in Christ, one of the first things we share is that they must be prepared for the attacks of Satan. He's never happy when a person chooses Christ over the world, and he'll use their first days and weeks in the faith to try to stunt their growth. If they live in a hostile environment, it's important to talk about the need for wisdom in how they share and show their new faith. Ultimately, however, we're trusting them into the hands of the Lord for wisdom and protection.

I have known many who have lost jobs and family for the cause of Christ. Some have left their home country out of fear. Others, however, have remained, stood firm, and persevered, despite rejection. There is no one-size-fits-all response or picture of the persecuted Christian. I do know, however, that God does not forget them in their suffering. The faith chapter makes this clear. Read Hebrews 11:35–40. It's clear that even with all the suffering and persecution the faithful faced, they stood apart, willing to wait in hope for God to fulfill his promises. Because of that, the writer says, "The world was not worthy of them" (v. 38).

Those who know the sufferings of Christ in a personal way give testimony to the glory of God in ways many of us never can. They have the privilege of identifying with Jesus through rejection, abuse, torture, and even death. Why should I be the one to deny them that, if God chooses to use them in such a way?

The other side of persecution.

A dear brother, who has known persecution and imprisonment for his faith, is a constant reminder to me that sufferings may be seasonal. In the early years of his faith he was a bold evangelist, traveling to many countries to share Christ. During this time, he was blacklisted from his own country and imprisoned in another. He has lost his family and all he knew, yet today he spends most of his time either traveling to areas where he can preach openly to reach Muslims for Christ or discipling groups in other countries via the internet and social platforms. Has he suffered? Yes. Has it stopped him from sharing Christ? Absolutely not.

When the devil wants us to be frozen in our fear of sharing, he gets us to focus on the moment. God always has the big picture in mind. Read Romans 8:18 and 2 Corinthians 4:16-18. Turn your eyes to Jesus, who suffered and died for our sin, that we might live without fear and for his glory. This is the message the world needs to hear, no matter the cost.

For Further Meditation

Ask the Holy Spirit to search your heart to reveal the reasons behind your fear of sharing your faith with those around you. Put it all out on the table before him, that he will free you from the worry and anxiety and renew you with boldness. Meditate on the words of Psalm 10:12–18, and pray them back to the Lord. Work through Hebrews 11, thinking about the impact of those who have suffered for their faith.

Day 27

I Feel Spiritually Abused

*Even my friend in whom I trusted,
one who ate my bread,
has raised his heel against me.*
Psalm 41:9

"I feel like I'm in the middle of a soap opera. My supervisor is telling leadership one thing, but I know what's happening on the ground. Last week he used ministry funds for a personal trip for his family. When our local partner offered to go with them to do the 'outreach' he was claiming to be doing, I heard him lie right to the man's face. He told him this was just a trip to check out the area for future outreaches, so he didn't need him along for this but would take him later. When our partner looked at me, I just shrugged and kept my mouth closed. My supervisor later cornered me in his office and told me to keep my mouth shut about this. His family needed this time away, and he would be scoping out the area. Yeah, right."

"I trusted them. They are my coworkers, my supervisors, my mentors. We are on the same team, serving the same purpose; and yet, this is not right. Their attitudes toward the nationals are awful, and they are expecting me to agree with them on everything they propose or do. How can I when it goes against the Word, not to mention against our organization's policy? If I question their opinions or actions, I'm humiliated before my colleagues. Then there was the way one of them acted toward me in private. I've never been so uncomfortable in my life. I'm not sure what to do or where to turn."

Help Me, Lord!

How Can I Share If It Threatens Their Lives?

Church life is messy.

Did you ever see a letter to a church where Paul or Peter or John said, "You're doing a great job—keep it up!"? Unfortunately, no, but thankfully, we have letters full of warnings and rebukes. Why? Because the church is made up of imperfect people, and church life is messy. And by now you know that what happens in church life carries over to mission or team life.

I remember the first time I sat in a team meeting after years of putting every missionary I knew and had prayed for on a pedestal. I was shocked that such holy people could become so unglued about issues and be so hateful toward each other. I'd say that most pedestals were cracked or completely knocked over that day. It was discouraging until my own pedestal took a beating as well; then I knew the reality of ministry life—we're all imperfect people trying our best to serve a perfect God. We're going to mess up.

Once settled on the fact that we're all just cracked pots, I had to face the next reality check—not everyone has the same background. While I came from a fairly stable Christian home, for which I counted my blessings, not everyone does. We all have baggage, whether it's a troubled home life or sitting under the instruction of a poor Bible teacher. And there are a lot of things that can boil to the surface when a person moves to a new culture or begins to work full-time in ministry. Unfortunately, when those things rise up, they almost always have a negative effect on others.

> I urge Euodia and I urge Syntyche to agree in the Lord. Yes, I also ask you, true partner, to help these women who have contended for the gospel at my side, along with Clement and the rest of my coworkers whose names are in the book of life. (Phil 4:2–3)

When opinions differ, tempers flare and discord reigns. If you're struggling with disagreements between you and another team member, pray and then go to them to see if you can work it out. If not, bring in a third coworker who is respected by both of you.

Handling conflicts.

Even Jesus knew there would be conflicts in the body. After all, he knows us better than we know ourselves. Thankfully, he gave us clear guidelines for handling conflicts in Matthew 18:15–20.

As with a difference of opinion, a true conflict, where you've been hurt by a fellow believer, requires action on your part. Some people are so forceful and direct in their speaking that they are unaware of any harm they cause when disagreeing or trying to impose their view on another. Thus, the importance of going to them alone and sharing your hurt is crucial, as you offer them grace by providing an opportunity to repent or offer an apology.

If this does not provide reconciliation and restoration, then get one or two coworkers to go with you. If the issue is not resolved, then the entire team must be involved to make a decision and direct it to leadership. The solution Jesus offers to the church applies as well to our mission teams. If this is your struggle, and you've been hurt by a brother or sister, then prayerfully work through these steps.

Handling counterfeiters.

While we can be hurt through the words or actions of colleagues, sometimes teams discover they have a true counterfeiter in their midst. Because most organizations do a thorough job of interviewing and vetting candidates for service, this is rare, but it's not out of the realm of possibility.

In my thirty years of ministry I have really only experienced this once, when a colleague with another group but who was working closely with us began teaching counter to Scripture. As a result, there was much confusion among the young believers and those considering accepting Christ. After my husband talked with him, we ended up having to disassociate in order to save the work and maintain our integrity. We knew this could happen. Paul wrote about it in 2 Corinthians 11.

What was Paul's counter to the counterfeiters? Humbling himself and elevating the gospel. He purposefully lived and spoke in such a way that those who were hearing the message would find nothing against him. Integrity goes a long way in shining light on false teaching.

Prayer is integral to having wisdom in how to speak to and stop the work of a counterfeit minister in your midst. Also, do not do it alone. You need mature believers with you in this effort in order not to hinder the work. The ones who suffer most in such cases are the young believers and those who are just hearing about Christ. Do all you can to protect them.

Physical or emotional abuse.

I purposefully did not use the word *handling* for this part, because when suffering comes as a result of abuse, we seldom feel like we're simply handling it. Abuse of any form by a colleague or fellow believer is devastating and requires strength to turn to others for help. The body of Christ is meant for times like this, and as much as it hurts or you feel personal shame as a result of another's words or actions, this is no time to try to go it alone.

Admitting you've been the victim of abuse on any level is the first step toward healing, and the Lord uses brothers and sisters in Christ to help us in that process. If you're part of an organization, there should be an emergency number for you to call or a member care representative who can be your first point of contact. If you're not able to do this, then have a trusted colleague do it for you. Don't sit in your hurt. Reach out as soon as you can.

God is with us in our trials, and if you've been the victim of an abusive colleague or believer, he sees you and will rescue you. Turn to him in prayer and turn to colleagues for help.

For Further Meditation

Conflicts and trials are refining tools God uses to grow us further into the likeness of Christ. No one is immune from the ugliness of the sinful nature of man, and when we're struck by a blow of ungodliness in another, we must turn to Christ to find purpose in the pain. The pain is real, just as that of the cross was real for Christ, but he is able to restore the years the locusts have eaten. Meditate on Joel 2:25–32, Psalm 41, Psalm 69. Let your hurts and your praises be made known to the God who sees.

Day 28

Why Do My Kids Have to Leave?

*In the fear of the Lord one has strong confidence
and his children have a refuge.*
Proverbs 14:26

"I've really been struggling with missing my kids. Two are at boarding school and one just left for college, and I'm stuck here with our youngest. I couldn't believe it when my single colleague decided to take some vacation days and stay near the boarding school. I'm very happy she can spend some time with my girls, but what about me? I want to go so bad, but my husband tells me I'm needed here. It's a busy time for our team; I get that, but I'm overwhelmed with this loss I have for my kids. I'm missing so much in their lives."

"Don't you promise safety in the center of your will? How can it be safe for me but not for my kids? I don't get why they have to be in another country for school. They are so young. Who will protect them if I'm not there? They seem happy, which bothers me even more. Don't they want to stay here? Don't they miss me? Are things that tough for them here? The oldest is just starting college in a land which is not really his home. He knows nothing about America. I'm really worried that the wrong people will influence him. I never thought that obeying your call would mean giving up my kids."

Help Me, Lord!

Why Do My Kids Have to Leave?

Family is God's design.

When God created woman and brought her to the man, the first family was formed. Over and over again in Scripture, we know that the Lord calls man to be fruitful and multiply. Family is also the perfect illustration of our relationship with God as our heavenly Father. We live as family in the church—brothers and sisters in Christ. God knows about family. It was his idea.

God also knows the responsibility and emotions of parents. He relates to parents in several verses of Scripture (Isa 49:15; 66:13; 2 Cor 6:18; Ps 68:5). He has the compassion and comfort of mothers. He is a father to us all. If you are hurting over having to let your child go, know that the Father feels your pain and understands your grief.

Following Christ has a cost.

Jesus's words are hard to hear when we're faced with the reality of sending a child out of the city or country for school.

> *Now great crowds were traveling with him. So he turned and said to them, "If anyone comes to me and does not hate his own father and mother, wife and children, brothers and sisters—yes, and even his own life—he cannot be my disciple. Whoever does not bear his own cross and come after me cannot be my disciple.* (Luke 14:25–27)

Are you hating your children for the sake of Christ? Hardly. But you are trusting God to care for those you love when you put him first in your life. I cannot help but think of Hannah. She longed for a child. Prayed earnestly for a child. She so trusted God for a child to the point that she was willing to offer his gift to her back to him in service (1 Sam 1:11).

Hannah saw her son once a year after she left him in the care and service of Eli, the priest. Did God watch over Samuel? Yes. Was his life without troubles? No. I'm sure caring for an elderly priest and his wicked sons was not easy. I'm sure he missed his mother, but God had his own plan for Samuel, which he also has for your children. Sometimes he uses the hardships of life through separation from parents to prepare children for the purpose they will fulfill in the future.

Just as Hannah gave up her son and entrusted him to God, so did the mother of Moses, Jochebed. She lived in a dangerous time as a Hebrew woman, when the king of Egypt ordered the midwives to kill any newborn Hebrew boys (Exod 1:15–17).

Moses was one of those boys. Destined to be killed if caught by the ruler of the day, his mother protected him by letting him go, not to school, but into the unknown upon the river, as she placed him in a basket. The school of experience for Moses would be in the household of Pharaoh's daughter, far away from the teaching of his parents, but this was the place God chose to prepare him to lead the Hebrews out of Egypt.

Reflect on two other women: Mary and Elizabeth. Each one had a son in a miraculous way, but each one would be required to give her son over to the Lord for special service. I'm sure Elizabeth grieved as she watched John turn away from all worldly things and head to the wilderness. She most likely worried about his health, as he was known for eating locusts and honey. Mary would make the ultimate sacrifice, watching her son turn his back on his earthly father's occupation to become a traveling rabbi and preacher. His decision would cost him his life on the cross—witnessed by his mother.

After considering the hearts of these mothers, remember the father who, in obedience to God, offered up his son on the altar—Abraham (Heb 11:17–19). The Lord knows the cost parents have paid over the centuries to obediently follow his will. He knows and is able to provide grace for the sacrifice because he first offered his only Son on our behalf. He willingly sent his Son to earth, becoming a man, limiting his presence by taking on flesh, denying himself the intimate fellowship they had known before time began. He did this that we might know him.

There is a cost in following the Lord, but God can redeem the price you pay by preparing your child for a future of his making. He showed us the way.

God sees and honors your sacrifice.

The Lord honored Hannah's sacrifice with more children. He honored Jochebed's offering of her son by putting him in the hands of a woman who would care for him and allow Jochebed time to nurse him until he was weaned. God sees and will honor your sacrifice. Jesus told his disciples that everyone who has sacrificed family or homes for the sake of the gospel will "receive a hundred times more," along with eternal life (Matt 19:28–30).

The Lord has plans for your child, just as he has plans for you (Jer 29:11–13). You may feel like you or your child is in exile, but in either case God is with you both. He has a hope and a future prepared for each of you, and it is good. Rest in that.

For Further Meditation

Study the lives of those mentioned in this chapter. Ask the Lord how you can respond as any one of them to this hard time in your life. In your hurt, cry to the Lord, using the Psalms. Work through Psalm 86, Psalm 78:1–8, and Psalm 8. Seek the Lord's counsel on how you can teach your children from afar, being reminded of God's commands to his people in Deuteronomy 11.

Day 29

I Can't Help This Bitterness

> *Pursue peace with everyone, and holiness—*
> *without it no one will see the Lord. Make sure that no one falls*
> *short of the grace of God and that no root of bitterness springs up,*
> *causing trouble and defiling many.*
> Hebrews 12:14–15

"I am so done with this country and its people. I walked into an office the other day to check on my husband, and I heard a man tell the women who were with him that I was unclean. He didn't know I understood him, but I did. Just because I didn't cover my long hair! Then a kid hit me with a rock while I was walking with friends in another part of town. What have I done to them? It's not easy to be just with women, and I have to get out of the house sometimes, don't I? But all of this is making me just want to stay home. It's not worth it!"

"I am so underappreciated. I answer the phone or make visits at all times of the day or night. These people never hesitate to throw their needs at me to fix. Whether it's help with a visa or a question about the Bible, apparently, I'm the go-to man. The problem is, they never ask about me: how I'm doing, or if I have needs. They never say "Thank you" for anything. It's just a constant giving without any recognition. I'm done!"

"I've never been in such a place or among such a people. The hardness of their hearts puts up walls to even the smallest effort to share the truth of Christ or to even do good in his name. They want nothing to do with me. Living here is unbearable; everything is hard to accomplish, even the simplest of tasks. I had such fellowship with the body of Christ before we came here. Now it's all gone, and I'm just left with bitterness and despair."

Help Me, Lord!

Bitterness comes when the soil is poisoned.

Though our minds know the truth, it's not easy to get out of the trap of bitterness once we've let it grow and flourish. Fellowship with the Lord does not depend on place or people but on our openness for him to speak and fill us with his Spirit. Some of the sweetest fellowship with the Lord is in the desert places of life. It can only be sweet, however, when we take our eyes off our surroundings and look to him for the bread of life.

Where does bitterness start? In our minds. We have a hard day, and a bad attitude takes root. Instead of turning to the Lord and his Word before we sleep, we crash and burn in exhaustion. What happens the next morning? We carry that attitude into the new day, letting it affect all we do and see and how we respond to new trials or struggles. Before we know it, our mind is poisoned with the hopelessness that Satan wants us to feel, and a bitterness for not having what we once knew rises up.

David felt and wrote about this in Psalm 13. His anxious concerns and anguish were getting stored up in his mind. They weren't going anywhere; they were putting down roots within him. Bitterness and despair promote an anxious heart and agony of the mind. This state of mind is just where Satan wants us to stay. He's got you down until you remember the Lord, in whom you trust.

Illness can be another crack in our spiritual armor that Satan uses to pierce us with bitterness. King Hezekiah was terrified and had turned bitter as a result of a debilitating illness (Isa 38:2–3). When illness hits us in service, we question God's call and wonder why we surrendered in the first place. Like Hezekiah, we sometimes become bitter because we look at *our* sacrifice instead of what God might be trying to teach us through this trial.

The prophet Isaiah offered hope to the king, which led Hezekiah to write a poem after his recovery (Isa 38:9–20). He recognized that he had let the illness open the door to bitterness, but with thanksgiving his relationship with the God who healed him was restored. Hezekiah is not the best example for understanding bitterness, because he did not recognize the selfish motives in his response to the illness. He does, however, praise the Lord for bringing him through the trial, giving him thanks for his deliverance.

When bitterness has you in its grip, search your heart. Where did it start? With a small offense, a bad day, an illness, rejection, or loss? Go back to the beginning in your mind and heart and begin to confess and clean out the soil of self that is giving fertilizer to bitterness of soul.

Hard tasks need to be accepted with a grateful heart.

Ezekiel had it rough. He was in exile with God's people. He knew the Lord and was obviously a man of righteousness, because he'd been called to speak on God's behalf. He was granted the privilege of seeing things others could only dream of seeing. But now God wanted him to get off the proverbial mountain and deliver a harsh message to a rebellious people. It was their fault they were living in exile in the first place. Ezekiel was not a happy camper (Ezek 3:10–15). It left him bitter and angry.

Have you just sat, stunned that you're actually having to live in such a place and among such a people? That was Ezekiel. He'd been in the presence of the Lord! He'd tasted a scroll that was sweet as honey. He'd seen the brilliance of the throne of God. Now he was relocated to the valley; and though he spoke the same language as these people, which should have made the job easier, it was hardly that, because their hearts were hard and they didn't want to hear what he had to say.

Still, he obeyed the Lord and did the hard thing God had asked of him. His was a hard, hard ministry and included a lot of words of condemnation. In the midst of his service, Ezekiel's wife died, and God tells him not to mourn or cry. This was to be a sign to the people. He would have to prophesy from the valley of dry bones to the hope of new life and return by the Spirit.

If Ezekiel had remained in his bitterness, stunned and frozen in his faith, we would not have the hope of the final words of his prophecy (Ezek 48:30–35). Instead, because of his obedience, he left his people and us, not only the dimensions, not only the dimensions of the City of God, but the promise that its name would proclaim "The Lord Is There."

We praise God for those mountaintop moments, for they are what carry us through the valleys. Don't let the vine of bitterness ensnare you on the way down the road of service.

Change the pH level of the soil of bitterness by adding thanksgiving.

I spent one year writing each day one reason to be thankful. It was after the loss of my husband, and I was going through some struggles in ministry. On some days, I felt like I was forcing myself to find a reason to be grateful, and even though it was hard, it was always possible. God worked in my heart that year, moving me through my grief and trial. I became a grateful person because I willfully chose to seek out reasons to be thankful.

When we're surrounded by evil, it can be easy to let a bitter attitude lead us to neglect those we're called to serve. This is not the way of Christ. We are to pursue good for others, and as we do, rejoice in what God is doing in our own heart as well as theirs. Cover every interaction you have with prayer (1 Thess 5:15–19). Pray for the good of the people among whom you live, and give thanks in everything. When we let bitterness be our guide, the Spirit is stifled. He's still there, but he can't work freely and to his fullest in us. Thankfulness unlocks the door for him to return.

Just as you pray for those who are suffering, seek prayer when you are feeling strangled by bitterness (Jas 5:13). Get your prayer partners and accountability partners busy, letting them walk beside you in the dark days. Thank God for those who pray for you, knowing he will hear and answer them on your behalf, even when you're struggling to pray yourself.

Finally, when the Lord brings you through the tunnel of bitterness into the joy of service once again, give thanks and testify to the work of the Lord in your life. Just as Hezekiah praised the Lord for his recovery, praise him for yours. Your testimony of God's goodness in the midst of your personal struggles can touch and bring hope to others who are bearing the weight of a bitter heart.

For Further Meditation

Read and meditate on the words of the prophet Jeremiah in Lamentations. Focus especially on chapter 3—to be reminded of God's great love for you, which keeps you from being consumed. His mercies are truly new every morning and his compassion never fails. Put your hope in him.

Day 30

This Loss Is Too Painful

*Even when I go through the darkest valley,
I fear no danger,
for you are with me;
your rod and your staff—they comfort me.*
Psalm 23:4

"I am having bad dreams. Each one is about a person dying. From my husband, to my parents, to my only brother. I can't seem to get death off my mind. The losses I've dealt with have increased the anxiety in my heart. I have a problem leaving my kids at school. I am fearful something will happen to them. The people of this country seem to take death so easily. Fate or God wills it, so they have to accept it. How can a mother who just lost a child to malaria be back to work the next week, like nothing happened? I could never do that."

"My father died last month. I'm thankful I got to go home to be with my mother and siblings, but now I'm back and struggling. Dad was my rock in so many ways, but as an adult and missionary, I thought I would handle his death better. I know that people are watching me in my grief, so I'm trying to be strong, but it's hard. I'm beginning to wonder if I need to go home. Maybe Mom needs me, and being with her will help me work through this."

"Our cat died this week, and it's made me lose total control. What's wrong with me? It's just a cat, yet somehow it's brought up loss that I thought I'd dealt with before we even left for the field. The hurt from our miscarriage and the loss of our sister. Then I remembered my grandmother's death last year. Why couldn't we go back and be with family? Maybe this cat dying was just the last straw."

Help Me, Lord!

This Loss Is Too Painful

Loss can suck the life out of us.

The source of the loss doesn't matter—it's all painful, and even that which seems insignificant in the eyes of the world can trigger the greater sense of loss we're already feeling by living away from family and the familiar. Thankfully, we can give voice to the hurt through God's Word. Psalm 88 captures the pain that wells up in times of grief. More than once, the psalmist says, "I cry out to you" or "I call to you for help."

Loss hurts. Loss pulls us down. Loss wears us out.

God hears us in our loss.

When we think we can't go on, God is there to lift us out of our grief and loss. His ears are open to our cries for help (Ps 34:15). The risen Christ will not leave us in the valley of the shadow of death, but comes alongside us, as "a man of suffering, and familiar with pain" (Isa 53:3 NIV). Our grief is never too deep for Christ to intervene and save, for he knows death and cried at the loss of his own friend, Lazarus (John 11:35).

Grief can bring all the temptations of comparison and self-pity to the surface with amazing speed. God knows our weaknesses, even as he holds us in the pain. Again, acknowledging our weakness to him, even when we can't acknowledge it to those around us, opens the door to healing. When he had become bitter and felt wounded in his soul, the psalmist remembered the most important thing. In the midst of grief, God is the only one we have and desire. He alone will renew our strength.

> *Who do I have in heaven but you?*
> *And I desire nothing on earth but you.*
> *My flesh and my heart may fail,*
> *but God is the strength of my heart,*
> *my portion forever.*
> *Those far from you will certainly perish;*
> *you destroy all who are unfaithful to you.*
> *But as for me, God's presence is my good.*
> *I have made the LORD God my refuge,*
> *so I can tell about all you do.* (Ps 73:25–28)

We grieve, but not without hope.

Even death and loss can be an opportunity for God to be glorified, as we yield to his purposes and sovereignty. When a family member or local believer passes away, Paul's words to the church in Thessalonica are important to speak, not only to ourselves but to those who come to offer condolences. We grieve for those in Christ, but not without hope (1 Thess 4:13–15). This life is not the end. God comforts us with this reality and also helps us find the strength to proclaim it to others.

The death of Lazarus was just such an opportunity for Jesus (John 11:4), as he told the crowd that the death of his friend had a purpose—for the Son of God to be glorified. There were tears and grief and the struggles of the two sisters, but ultimately God had the last word. He will have the last word with those we lose as well. We may not see it through a miraculous healing in the moment, but we will see it through the miraculous healing at Christ's return. Rest in that hope. Rejoice and find comfort in that hope.

God will restore our souls.

When we're in the middle of grief, there seems to be no end in sight. Darkness weighs us down in the valley, even as we seek comfort and rest in God's Word. As we allow him to walk with us through our grief, the fog begins to lift—not suddenly, but gradually, as we put one foot in front of the other and move forward in life. Don't let guilt overwhelm you when you realize you've smiled or laughed again, or found yourself humming a song. These are signs of restoration, and they are from the Lord.

> *I will repay you for the years*
> *that the swarming locust ate,*
> *the young locust, the destroying locust,*
> *and the devouring locust—*
> *my great army that I sent against you.* (Joel 2:25)

Just like a locust swarm, grief seems to eat and destroy everything in its path. Our God is able to restore the days, the months, and even the years that grief has taken from us.

When death comes our way in the loss of family members, friends, colleagues, or church members, we put our hurt and grief into God's hands. In doing so, God receives the glory even in these hard times of life. Ministry may slow for a season, but healing and the opportunity to testify to the Lord's goodness and presence during loss is sure to come.

This Loss Is Too Painful

For Further Meditation

Pore over Psalm 88, underlining the words that describe the state of your heart. Make them your heart cry to the Lord. As you rest in the knowledge that he hears you, begin to thank him that he is the God who "heals the brokenhearted and bandages their wounds" (Ps 147:3).

Conclusion

Where do you go from here? That is between you and the Lord. If you are honest with yourself, you'll realize that the struggles and questions raised in this book are not of the one-and-done variety. Many will come back, and you'll find Satan working to derail you once again from your call and purpose. Don't let him. Return to the days and Scriptures needed to restore your balance and relationship with the Lord.

Along with continuing to use this book as a resource for prayer and growth, I encourage you to turn to a few other ideas that can also help.

Thanksgiving

Find ways to see the blessings of each day, whether you write them in a journal, post them on your bathroom mirror, or voice them in your prayers. Maintaining an attitude of gratitude is key to keeping bitterness at bay. If you live with family members or a roommate, choose to voice what you're thankful for each day during mealtime.

Thanking God for even the smallest of blessings changes our mindset and readjusts our attitudes, giving us extra encouragement to keeping our eyes open to what he's doing and how he's showing us grace.

Accountability

If you don't have an accountability partner, get one. We all need someone to whom we can turn when we are struggling or facing challenges in service. If you have an accountability partner but haven't been good at connecting with them, mark your calendar for regular calls, emails, or visits. Even if you aren't facing a big issue at the moment, accountability checks on your quiet time, exercise, sleep, or budgeting finances are all important and help us maintain a balance in life and service.

Conclusion

Looking Outward

If this book has helped you, you can be assured that there are others in your team, family, or home church who are struggling with questions and ministry. I've often been able to work through my own trials while encouraging others in theirs. As you've been able to press forward in service despite the questions and troubles, you can speak into the lives of others who are struggling. Ask the Lord to use what he's taught you through his Word to speak into the life of a colleague or family member.

As you serve, leaning on the Lord for his help when trials come, remember his words to Abraham, after Sarah laughed at the thought of having a child at such an advanced age:

Is anything impossible for the Lord? (Gen 18:14)

Whatever you face, the God of the possible is able to see you through. He is the God who longs to show you grace and give you his peace. Rest in him.

About the Author

After serving over twenty years in cross-cultural ministry, Carol returned with her family to the United States and found a new role in writing and speaking about missions, Islam, cross-cultural living, and the Christian life. Along with her service at the Arabic-language church she and her late husband founded, Carol worked for more than a decade as the manager of her local public library. Now retired, Carol focuses on writing projects, including an active blog at lifeinexile.net. Maggie, her loyal cat, has a special spot on her desk.

In addition to her books, Carol is a contract writer for *Missions Mosaic* magazine and has contributed to several collaborative works, including *Muslim Conversions to Christ* and the Beth Moore *Voices of the Faithful* series.

To find a complete list of Carol's books or to schedule her for a speaking engagement, visit lifeinexile.net.

WILLIAM CAREY PUBLISHING
visit us at missionbooks.org

Bags Packed, Hearts Ready: Stories of God's Faithfulness in Cross-Cultural Ministry
Sue Eenigenburg

In *My Bags Packed, Hearts Ready,* Sue Eenigenburg shares heartfelt reflections that delve into her experiences as a cross-cultural worker and mother. Through personal anecdotes, humor, and scriptural insight, she reveals how grace, gratitude, and trust in God can transform even the most challenging times into testimonies of divine provision and strength. Each story in this book ends with questions and a space to reflect and pray.

Great Commission Spirituality: Abiding in Christ, Serving in Obscurity
E. D. Burns

In *Great Commission Spirituality,* E. D. Burns skillfully unfolds the peace-giving assurance of our union with Christ. This weighty truth provides not only the foundation but also the force behind our endeavors, allowing us to labor with confidence even in barren fields. By emphasizing that Christ lives in and works through us, Burns reassures readers that true fruitfulness in ministry comes from abiding in Christ, who orchestrates our work by his Word and perfect timing.

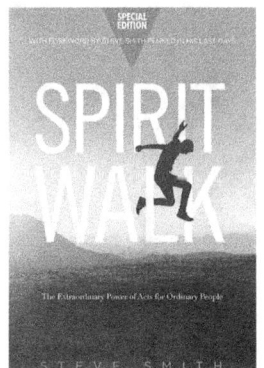

Spirit Walk (Special Edition): The Extraordinary Power of Acts of Ordinary People
Steve Smith

Though we know the Bible says to walk in the Spirit, the majority of Christians are illiterate (and even nervous) about how to practically live in His power. The result is lives marred by continued brokenness and ministries plagued by fruitlessness. In contrast, believers from Acts understood the ancient path of the Spirit Walk. That extraordinary power was not just for them, but also for us. Whether you need a movement of God in your personal life or in your ministry, this book takes you through the timeless principles of the Bible.

www.ingramcontent.com/pod-product-compliance
Lightning Source LLC
Chambersburg PA
CBHW052146070526
44585CB00017B/1996